RIMEY LAMA CHOPA

A Tibetan Rimey Tantric Feast

A Rite to Invoke
the Supreme Nectar of Wisdom

Kyapje Dilgo Khyentse Rinpoche

Badgodra, India

1975

RIMEY LAMA CHOPA
A Tibetan Rimey Tantric Feast

A Rite to Invoke
the Supreme Nectar of Wisdom

Composed by

Dilgo Khyentsey Rinpoche

at the request of Trulzhik Rinpoche

Translated into English by
Glenn H. Mullin

Foreword by
Ven. Matthieu Ricard

ᚼSUMERU

RIMEY LAMA CHOPA
A Tibetan Rimey Tantric Feast
A Rite to Invoke the Supreme Nectar of Wisdom

Dilgo Khyentsey Rinpoche
Translated by Glenn H. Mullin

Translation © Glenn H. Mullin 2010
All rights reserved

Design by Karma Yönten Gyatso

Cover & Frontispiece photos
© Matthieu Ricard/Shechen Archives

Published by
The Sumeru Press Inc.
PO Box 2089, Richmond Hill, ON
Canada L4E 1A3

ISBN 978-1-896559-05-6 (print edition)

For more information about The Sumeru Press
visit us at *www.sumeru-books.com*

50% of profits from sales of this book go towards humanitarian
projects in the Himalayas supported by Rinpoche's charitable
foundation. For more information about their work, visit them
at *www.karuna-shechen.org*

Contents

Acknowledgements

I would very much like to thank Roberto Sanchez of the Rimey Center in Chicago (formally known as the Rime Foundation of Chicato), who in 1995 requested me to translate Dilgo Khyentse's Rimey Lama Chopa for use by their Sangha. I had taught at the Rimey Center whenever my annual lecture and workshop tours took me through the Mid-West, and I was delighted to have the opportunity to immerse myself in Rinpoche's wonderful text.

I would also very much like to thank the various lamas and Dharma friends who assisted me with the project. Verse works are never easy to translate. Many ideas, terms and names are condensed into metered lines, with many abbreviations. In addition, whenever Rinpoche refers to any doctrine in any of the eight main sects that his text focuses on, he uses terminology unique to that school.

I was based in Nepal at the time, and had the good fortune that Geshey Gendun Zopa, a Rimey lama from Loseling Monastery in South India, happened to be in the country when I began the project. He was travelling with a young monk friend of mine, Geshey Ngawang Pendey. I made my first reading of the text with them, in a hermitage at Parping where they were staying at the time.

A few months later I approached a Bhutanese khenpo friend at Shechen, the monastery that Dilgo Khyentse had established in Nepal and where he resided until his passing in 1991. Khenpo referred me to Jangchub Lingpa (Jangling Tulku), a close personal disciple of Dilgo Khyentse, commenting that, "Although Jangling Tulku is young, he knows this text far better than I. He will be able to answer all questions and resolve all doubts." Khenpo's words proved more than true. Jangling Tulku graciously met with me once a day for the next month, and we steadily re-read the entire work.

Later I re-checked difficult passages with my old Dharma friend and fellow translator Keith Dowman, who is very well versed in Nyingma literature and terminology. Keith's interests lie more in dzogchen than in Buddhist ritual and liturgy, but he nonetheless took time to review and discuss thirty or so of the more obscure verses with me.

Finally, the very illustrious Ven. Matthieu Ricard, one of Dilgo Khyentse's foremost Western students, and a truly great Rimey monk, agreed to discuss several of the passages with me. This was back in 1995, when I made the first draft of the text.

More recently (2010), on the long bus ride from Kathmandu to Sarnath, Ven. Matthieu took the time to check over the entire work with Shechen Rabjam Tulku, Dilgo Khyentse's great Dharma heir. This kindness is beyond my powers of expression. I can only visualize the two of them bouncing along the bumpy Indian roads hour after hour, checking the English rendition against the Tibetan original.

Finally, I would like to thank John Negru of Sumeru Press in Canada for publishing the work.

Glenn H. Mullin
(Maitri Zopa)
January 3rd, 2011
Mongolia

Foreword

Over the centuries, following the appearances of preeminent masters, eight major spiritual lineages flourished in Tibet. It all began in the eighth century when King Trisong Deutsen (b. ca 742) invited the Indian abbot Shantarakshita to Tibet, and, soon afterward, the great master Padma Sambhava, who became known in the Land of Snows as "A Second Buddha." Padma Sambhava bestowed the ripening empowerments and liberating instructions upon the Tibetan king Trisong Deutsen, the dakini Yeshe Tsogyal and the other of his twenty-five main disciples. He entrusted many teachings to each of them and miraculously concealed these as spiritual treasures (terma) in various places—rocks, lake, temples, statues, and even in the sky. He then prophesied that, in the future, these disciples would reincarnate, reveal these teachings from their place of concealment at appropriate times and spread them for the sake of beings.

At the same time, Shantarakshita established in Tibet the monastic lineage as well as the philosophical tradition of the great Nalanda Monastery of Northern India. Under Padma Sambhava and Vimalamitra's guidance, over a hundred great Indian panditas and an equivalent number of Tibetan translators translated most of the Buddhist Canon from Sanskrit into Tibetan. This period is known as the Early Translation Period, or *Ngagyur*. The upholders of the vast and rich spiritual tradition that flourished in its wake are known as the Ancient Ones, or Nyingma.

Following the persecution waged by King Langdarma, the monastic lineage came close to eradication and survived thanks to five fully ordained monks (four Tibetan and one Chinese), who headed by Lachen Gonpa Rabsel were able to preserve the ordination lineage. At the same time the essential contemplative teachings survived through lineages of highly realized lay yogins.

In the late tenth century, a second great wave of translation began, spearheaded by the great translator Rinchen Sangpo (957-1055). The various lineages that sprang from it belong to the New Translation Period, or *Sargyur*.

Numerous Sarma or New Schools emerged including the Sakya, the Dvakpo Kagyu, the Shangpa Kagyu, the Zhiche and Chod, the Kalachakra or Jordrug, the Orgyen Nyengyu, and the Kadam, together with its later development, the Geluk.

These traditions, old and new, are often called the Eight Chariots of Spiritual Accomplishment (*Drub- gyu Shingta Gye*).

As these various lineages spread all over Tibet, they put more or less emphasis on either philosophical studies or contemplative practice; but all of them laid strong foundations in uniting study, reflection and meditation, as well as uniting within a single stream of personal practice the graded levels of the Three Vehicles: Hinayana, Mahayana and Vajrayana.

The Rimey approach of Buddhist philosophy and practice has existed throughout Tibetan history, but it became strongly emphasized at the end of the 19th century, at a time when many spiritual lineages had become weak, with tribal feuds and sectarianism dividing peoples and monasteries. Several great luminaries appeared at that time, spearheaded by Jamyang Khyentse Wangpo (1820-1892), Jamgon Kongtrul (1813-1899), Patrul Rinpoche (1808-1887) and Lama Mipham (1846-1912). They exemplified the ecumenical ideas of spiritual openness and "pure perception" (*dag nang*), that are characteristics of all genuine Buddhist practitioners.

A bit earlier, another inspiring example of a great master who perceived the deep unity of all traditions was given by Shabkar Tsogdruk Rangdrol (1781-1851), who combined the Sarma traditions of the altruistic Mind Training taught by Atisha (and developed by Tsongkhapa) with the practices of the Nyingma tradition. He wrote:

> In the snow-ranges of Tibet,
> Owing to the kindness of sublime beings of the past,
> Many profound teachings were taught.
> These days most practitioners
> Hold the various teachings to be contradictory,
> Like heat and cold.
> They praise some teachings, and disparage others.

Some holy beings have said that
Madhyamika, Mahamudra, and Dzogchen
Are like sugar, molasses, and honey:
One is as good as the other.
For this reason, I have listened to
And practiced all of them without partiality.

He was himself echoing other teachers such as Panchen Lobsang Yeshe (1663-1737, the 5th Panchen Lama and 2nd to hold the title "Panchen Lama") who said:

The various doctrinal views found in the provinces of U, Tsang, and Ngari Are all the very teachings of the Victorious One. How fine if, not allowing the demon of sectarianism to ignite animosity, The radiance of the jewel of pure perception would encompass all.

These masters did not merely receive teachings from all traditions of Tibetan Buddhism, but actively taught pure perception and unbiased open-mindedness. They eloquently explained how all the many different Dharma teachings of the various yanas form one coherent, non-contradictory whole. Gathering teachings from all areas of Tibet and from masters of all spiritual traditions, these teachers—themselves all authentic masters, scholars, poets, commentators, and accomplished yogins—saved the heritage of Tibetan Buddhism from decline and restored its vitality. This heritage still benefits us today.

Some of the essential teachings of the various traditions were compiled into major collections, such as the *Five Great Treasuries* (*Dzod Chen Nam Nga*) of Jamgon Kongtrul Lodro Thayey, Yonten Gyatso (1813-1899 also known under his Terton name Pema Tennyi Yundrung Lingpa; and the *Collection of Tantric Lineages* (*Gyud De Kuntu*) and *Collection of Tantric Sadhanas* (*Drubtab Kuntu*), collected and arranged by Jamyang Loter Wangpo (1847-1914), so that they could be practiced and transmitted to future generations.

Patrul Rinpoche (1808-1887) for instance would teach the Shantideva's *Guide to the Bodhisattva Way* (Skt. *Bodhicharyavatara*) according to various commentaries from the Geluk, Sakya, Kagyu and Nyingma traditions (this last being his principal personal affiliation), depending on his audience.

The expression "Rimey" is a contraction for *risu machadpa*, which can be loosely rendered as "not falling into any bias." The term is set in contrast to someone who has great bias and prejudice (*chog-ri chenpo*) towards other schools.

Jamyang Khyentse Wangpo (1820-1892), who is the principal lama used for visualization in the guru yoga section of the text herein translated, was a master of all the Tibetan Buddhist traditions. When he was twenty-one he traveled to central Tibet, where he took full monastic ordination at Mindroling Monastery. Thereafter he traveled widely and received teachings from more than 150 masters, traveling on foot for thirteen years and wearing out fifty pairs of boots. Khyentse Wangpo was considered to be an incarnation of Manjushri and of King Trisong Deutsen. He revealed many spiritual treasures (*terma*). In addition, he experienced many recollections of his past lives, and by means of these recollections he was able to revive some of the spiritual treasures that had been discovered by him in his former incarnations, but for which the texts had been lost and the transmission become extinct. He was said to be the "Seal of all Treasure Revealors."

He was also was the only masters to have ever received the Seven Modes of Transmission (*ka-bab dun*), which are: 1) Oral tradition (*ka-ma*) the early teachings passed on unbrokenly from master to disciple; 2) Earth Treasure (*sa-ter*), revealed by the Tertons; 3) Rediscovered Treasure (*yang ter*), revealed for the second time from a past treasure; 4) Mind Treasure (*gong ter*), revealed within the wisdom mind of the tertön; 5) Hearing Lineage (*nyan gyud*), received directly from an enlightened being; 6) Pure Vision (*dag nang*), received in a pure meditative experience; and 7) Recollection (*je dran*), which is associated with remembrances from a former life.

Upon his return to eastern Tibet, he bestowed all the transmission he had received upon Jamgon Kongtrul, who then organized these and many others teachings into his *Five Treasuries*.

At the age of thirty-seven, Khyentse Wangpo decided to put into practice all the teachings he had received, and therefore vowed he would never again cross the threshold of his room. He never left his room, staying there for the remaining thirty-five years of his life, practicing many teachings, and composing (together with Jamgon Kongtrul) commentaries and instructions for practices whose previous explanations had been lost. He had countless visions of deities and past masters, some of them blending vision with actual presence.

Once for instance, as Khyentse Wangpo was in strict retreat, his attendant heard someone else talking in the innermost room. Wondering who could thus have penetrated unnoticed inside his master's retreat, he peeped through the door curtain and saw Khyentse Wangpo in conversation with an old lama. After a while, when the attendant returned to take care of his master's needs, he asked him: "Who was this person who came into your retreat?" Khyentse Wangpo replied: "You saw him? That means you have quite a pure karma. This was Vimalamitra."

Before Khyentse Wangpo passed away in 1892, he prophesied that he would reappear in five forms, or emanations of his body, speech, mind, qualities and activities. At the start of the 20th century these incarnations emerged, and while all of them were great masters, two of them were particularly eminent: Dzongsar Khyentse Chokyi Lodro (1894-1959), the "activity incarnation" who was an especially outstanding teacher during the first half of the century, and Dilgo Khyentse Rinpoche (1910-1991), the "mind incarnation" who taught innumerable students during the second half of the century, including many prominent members of today's generation of teachers of all schools.

Dilgo Khyentse Rinpoche used to say that sectarian views could only arise from the lack of knowledge of the depth and breadth of the teachings of the various spiritual lineages and philosophical views that flourished in Tibet. He sincerely believed that anyone who would read through the *Treasury of Spiritual Instructions (Dam-ngag Rinpoche Dzod)*, in which Jamgon Kongtrul collected the essential contemplative teachings of the Eight Chariots of Spiritual Accomplishment, would easily understand that all these teachings are not only noncontradictory, but can all lead to the highest spiritual realization.

Dilgo Khyentse Rinpoche was born in 1910. Upon his birth, he was blessed by Mipham Rinpoche and later said that this blessing was the single most important event in his life. At Shechen, one of the six principal monasteries of the Nyingmapa school, he met his root teacher, Shechen Gyaltsap Rinpoche (1871-1926), who formally recognized and enthroned the young Dilgo Khyentse Rinpoche as the mind incarnation of Jamyang Khyentse Wangpo, and gave him countless teachings.

It was also at Shechen that Khyentse Rinpoche met Jamyang Khyentse Chokyi Lodro, his second main teacher, who had also come to receive teachings from Shechen Gyaltsap.

Khyentse Rinpoche himself was to become the archetype of the spiritual teacher, someone whose inner journey led him to an extraordinary depth of knowledge and enabled him to be, for whoever met him, a fountain of loving kindness, wisdom and compassion.

To achieve these extraordinary qualities, Khyentse Rinpoche spent more than twenty years in retreat, in remote hermitages and caves. After and in between his retreats, Khyentse Rinpoche worked constantly for the benefit of all living beings with tireless energy. He became one of the main teachers of His Holiness the Dalai Lama, of the Royal Family of Bhutan, and of countless disciples. He was thus a master among masters.

His knowledge of the enormous range of Tibetan Buddhist literature was probably unparalleled, and he inherited Jamyang Khyentse Wangpo's determination to preserve and make available texts of all traditions, particularly those in danger of disappearing.

Profoundly gentle and patient though he was, Khyentse Rinpoche's presence, his vastness of mind and powerful physical appearance, inspired awe and respect in all who met him. He passed away in 1991 and his remains were cremated near Paro in Bhutan, in November 1992, at a ceremony attended by some fifty thousand devotees.

Khyentse Rinpoche was someone whose greatness was totally in accord with the teachings he professed. However unfathomable the depth and breadth of his mind might seem, from an ordinary point of view he was an extraordinarily good human being. His only concern was the present and ultimate benefit of others. Here was a living example of what lay at the end of the spiritual path—the greatest possible inspiration for anyone thinking of setting out on the journey to enlightenment.

Khyentse Rinpoche was the perfect example of a Rimey master. Although his personal, most intimate practice was centered upon the Nyingma tradition, chiefly the Mindroling tradition of Orgyen Terdag Lingpa and the Longchen Nyingthig tradition of Jigme Lingpa, at the same time he was deeply committed to receive, preserve and transmit the teachings from all schools of Tibetan Buddhism. He was not just paying lip service to this ecumenical approach, but was deeply concerned by the need to prevent rare transmissions from becoming extinct and greatly saddened when realizing that the lineage for the transmission of certain texts and empowerments was about to vanish.

Until his passing away, he would often ask a simple old monk passing by to give him the transmission for a particular rare text, having found out that this monk was holding the transmission for it. He once send one of his disciples to a remote areas of Eastern Tibet, in Dzamthang, to receive the reading transmission of a rare volume of commentary upon the Kalachakra Tantra, so that he could then receive it himself from his student and spread the transmission in a wider way.

This concern also manifested through his efforts to reprint more than 400 volumes of important texts, including Jamgon Kongtrul's Five Treasuries, with the support of E. Gene Smith (1936-2010) who, among the Western Tibetan scholars, was himself a sterling and unequalled example of someone with fathomless knowledge about the literature and history of all schools of Tibetan Buddhism and selfless dedication to preserve this precious literature.

It is therefore understandable that Dilgo Khyentse Rinpoche, at the request of Kyabje Trulshik Rinpoche, wrote a complete set of prayers, praises and offering to the masters of the lineages of the Eight Great Chariots of Accomplishments.

The text is officially listed in Tibetan as *Thub bstan ris su ma chad pa'i skyes bu dam pa'i tshogs rjes su dran pas gsol ba gdab cing mchod bstod bya ba'i rim pa byin rlabs ye shes bdud rtsi'i mchog stsol* ("Invoking The Nectar Of Wisdom: Prayers, Praises and Offering [inspired by] the Remembrance of the Assembly of Supreme Beings from the Various Lineages of the Muni's Teachings").

Jamgon Kongtrul, in his 19th century classic *Treasury of Oral Transmissions*, wrote separate *Lama Chopa* rituals for each of the Eight Chariots. Moreover, many years earlier Dilgo Khyentse Rinpoche also wrote a short text of offering to the masters of these eighth schools. However, the *Rimey Lama Chopa* that is herein translated is the first such text which does so in an expanded way.

We are very grateful to Glenn Mullin to have taken upon himself the task of rendering this ritual into English, and thus making it available for the first time to countless practitioners around the world.

His poetic translation was first published in Nepal, along with several other works, on the most auspicious occasion of celebrating the 100th anniversary of Dilgo Khyentse Rinpoche's birth, in February 2010. On this occasion thousands of people, including hundreds of masters from the four main schools of Tibetan Buddhism, as well as foreign disciples of Rinpoche from twenty-five countries, gathered at Shechen Monastery in Baudanath for three days, with Dilgo Khyentse's *Rimey Lama Chopa* as the main focus of practice.

We are equally grateful to the Chicago Rimey Dharma Center and Roberto Sanchez to have made the request for this translation to be accomplished.

May it be dedicated to the temporary and ultimate benefit of all beings, and the long life of all the great masters of all lineages. In particular, may it be dedicated to the long life of His Holiness the XIVth Dalai Lama, the spiritual leader of all Tibetans, who more than anyone in this century has succeeded in demonstrating and promoting the Rimey movement and pure views not only towards all schools of Tibetan Buddhism but towards all major religions at large; and also be dedicated to the long life and success of the young reincarnation of Dilgo Khyentse, Yangsi Orgyen Tendzin Jigme Lhundrup. And may the Rimey sentiment be widely embraced by all genuine practitioners.

Ven. Matthieu Ricard
December 18, 2010
Shechen Tennyi Dargyeling Monastery
Nepal

Translator's Introduction

Tibetan Buddhism is rich not only in the sheer volume of its literature, but also in the large number of genres of writings that it produced.

An important category is that of spiritual liturgy, the material that is chanted during various rituals. This form of literature is highly revered by the Tibetans, and the collected works of almost all great lamas is rich in it. Some of Tibet's most devotional, mystical and popular poetry can be found in it.

Tibetan liturgical literature itself comes in a large variety of types, from mandala rites such as sadhanas, self-initiations and fire rites, to Dharmapala invocations and healings/exorcisms, to simple temple festival and celebratory music.

An important genre is that known in Tibetan as *Lama Naljor*, or in Sanskrit as *Guruyoga*, which is expanded on special occasions into *Lama Chopa*, or Gurpuja. Both of these genres could be termed "meditation with chanting." The latter of the two is usually performed in conjunction with a tsok, or "tantric feast/celebration." Most monasteries perform a rite of this kind once or twice a month, usually on the tenth and twenty-fifth days of the lunar cycle. Each sect has its own cycle of texts related to the practice, and many of the larger monasteries have their individual traditions.

The Lama Chopa liturgy that is herein translated was written by the late great Dilgo Khyentse Rinpoche, one of the greatest Nyingma lamas to come out of Tibet. It is an excellent example of the tone and style of the Lama Chopa practices, and demonstrates through its poetry and imagery just why the Tibetans so love community rituals such as these. Rinpoche was regarded as one of the most talented and inspired masters of his generation, and his work here demonstrates why.

He gives us the context of his composition in the text's colophon:

When I was fifteen years old there was a gathering of many great masters, including the tantric lord of a hundred lineages, Padma Tenzin Khedrup Gyatso Wangpo Dey (i.e., the Third Sechen

Gyaltsap), accompanied by two young Jamgon incarnations (Matthieu comments: This refers to Dzongsar Jamyang Khyentse Chokyi Lodro, 1893-1959, and Shechen Kongtrul Pema Drime, 1901-1960). The lama gave extensive teachings at Zhechen Ritro Demchok Tashi Gepel Monastery on the subject of "The Treasury of Oral Instructions" (an important Rimey compilation). My name, Mangal, appeared on the list of attendees. Because of the kindness of this great master, I developed profound faith in the Buddhist Rimey movement.

Then when I was in my thirty-second year I received a small blessing from the chariots of the eight great practice lineages. Deeply moved by that experience, I composed a brief guruyoga liturgy focusing on them.

Later His Eminence Zhadeu Trulzhik Choktrul Gyurmey Chokyi Lodro Rinpoche (i.e. the great Trulshik Rinpoche, of the Mt. Everest region), a master who has truly aroused the perfections of the transmission and realization Dharmas within his stream of being, and who is a great upholder of the Rimey tradition, made the request that I compose a Lama Chopa practice text for Rimey practitioners. In response to his entreaty, I took the guruyoga text on the chariots of the eight practice lineages that I had previously composed, and somewhat expanded upon it, basing this on the writings of earlier masters, until it came into its present shape.

The key expression in the above passage is "Rimey," often translated as "non-sectarian," but which literally means something like "non-partisan," "un-biased," or "non-affiliated." The sense is "ecumenical." Thus "a Rimey lama" is a practitioner or teacher not linked exclusively to any one school, but rather who incorporates elements from all Tibetan Buddhist lineages in his/her daily spiritual endeavors. The term has been used over the centuries in conjunction with lamas who study, practice and teach lineages beyond the scope of the monastery (and thus the sect) to which they are most closely aligned, either by birth and family ties, monastic ordination, tantric initiation, and so forth.

As examples of great Rimey masters, Tibetans like to refer to the Second Dalai Lama, who during his lifetime was hailed as Zhaser Rimey Mawa, or

"The Yellow Hat Lama who Teaches without Affiliation" (i.e., a Gelukpa lama who teaches all doctrines and practices from all schools).

Another example is the Great Fifth Dalai Lama, who was a Gelukpa monk by monastic ordination, but studied, practiced and wrote on the doctrines of all schools. Dilgo Khyentse refers to him in the colophon of his text; in fact, Rinpoche even gives a liturgy with which the Great Fifth can be used to replace the main figure in the visualized assembly of the guruyoga section of the text (i.e., can be used to replace Jamyang Khyentse Wangpo).

Once the Fifth Dalai Lama was scolded by one of his tutors for studying too widely, and not dedicating enough time to his Gelukpa studies. He replied, "I am supposed to be the spiritual leader of all the Tibetans. To fulfill the role, I should at least know the teachings and practices of all the different sects, not just the one of my birth affiliation."

However, as the present Dalai Lama, himself a great embodiment of the Rimey tradition, once pointed out to me in an interview, it is important to understand that when the term "Rimey" is translated as "non-sectarian," this does not mean that those who chose not to follow the Rimey approach are sectarian in a negative sense. There is a "positive sectarianism," in that there will be many people who are better suited to dedicating themselves solely to the traditions of one particular school than they are to blending lineages. Blending, if not properly done, can lead to unproductive distraction and lack of both focus and structure. It is better to do one thing well than many things poorly. When properly done, an eclectic approach opens the doors to the world of ideas and tantric practices derived from the transmissions of all "eight great practice lineages."

Many years ago, for example, I translated for two American monks in an interview they had with the great Khamtrul Rinpoche, the head of the Drukpa Kargyu School in Kham. The monks asked Rinpoche for a tantric initiation. Rinpoche declined, with the reply, "It is better that you stick with one school. In that way you will get realization. By mixing, you will only get dilution of the blessings." Khamtrul Rinpoche himself was part of the Rimey movement, and over the years I received several initiations and transmissions from him. At one of them, Dilgo Khyentse, the author of the text herein translated, was present as co-transmitter. (The two took turns giving different parts of the transmission.) Yet Khamtrul Rinpoche advised those two particular monks against mixing lineages.

The Rimey movement received a major impetus in the mid-nineteenth century through the work of two lamas from Kham, Eastern Tibet. One of these was Jamyang Khyentse Wangpo, a Nyingmapa lama. The other was Jamgon Kongtrul the Great, a Karma Kargyupa luminary, whose prolific writings are regarded as some of the most brilliant of his generation. These two became close friends and colleagues, and under their efforts the Rimey movement went from being an informal approach to Dharma study and practice to becoming its own tradition, one in which the main elements of all the different schools can be integrated.

Dilgo Khyentse's Gurupuja text is an important window looking out to the work of Jamyang Khyentse Wangpo and Jamgon Kongtrul the Great.

The lama who stands in his liturgy as the central figure in the visualized lineages of gurus is Jamyang Khyentse Wangpo, the Nyingma lama who had so greatly contributed to the Rimey movement a century earlier; Jamgon Kongtrul is also there among the visualized assembly, and his name appears several times in Dilgo Khyentse's text.

The various lines of gurus that surround the central figure in the visualization (i.e. Jamyang Khyentse Wangpo), and thus symbolically whose teachings he had come to master and embody, represent the "eight great practice lineages" and "ten great teaching legacies." These are the historical rivers through which Buddhism and Buddhist culture became introduced into and spread throughout Tibet from India. The eight practice traditions were the essence, for they were constituted of the enlightenment teachings. The ten teaching traditions are also mentioned in Dilgo Khyentse Rinpoche's liturgy, because they provide the cultural tools for and a linguistic/intellectual environment conducive to the transmission of the enlightenment legacy.

The sections of his text with the list of names in the different lineages read like a Who's Who of Tibetan Buddhist history. All the early greats are there, from Padma Sambhava and Shantarakshita, to Atisha and Lama Drom, Marpa and Milarepa, Padampa Sanggye and Machik Labdron, the early Sakya lamas, the great treasure-text revealers, Tsongkhapa, the Dalai Lamas, and so forth. To the connoisseur Tibetologist, it is a feast of historical and mystical unfoldment.

Dilgo Khyentse Rinpoche's text contains all the standard phases of a Gurupuja practice manual, from visualization and invocation, to the six mindfulnesses of the guru's presence, the stages of outer, inner, secret and suchness offerings, the seven-limbed devotion, and so forth. The author brings his unique mystical and poetic genius into each of these.

Of particular interest is his handling of the eight practice lineages. The Rimey tradition is essentially a fusion of elements from these eight. Dilgo Khyentse goes through the eight several times, on each particular occasion using several code terms that are unique to the individual school, thus in effect introducing the philosophy and focus of each of the eight.

He mentions them first in the practice of the "six mindfullnesses of guruyoga," which is mindfulness of the guru's physical presence in the world. Here Jamyang Khyentse Wangpo is visualized in the center, with the gurus of the eight practice lineages around him. Several key historical names from each of the eight lineages are given. Rinpoche first gives a brief and then a more detailed liturgy (the latter to be dropped when time so requires). The latter is a banquet of tantric Buddhist historicity.

The eight are introduced again in the section of offering homage. Here Rinpoche often provides key names or terms with *chen*, or annotations, in which he gives additional information. Usually I have included these in brackets, though in some cases, where bringing them into the recited liturgy would be awkward, I have relegated them to footnotes.

The third appearance of the gurus of the eight lineages comes in the section with the third of the six mindfulness practices of guruyoga, i.e., mindfulness of the liberating lives of the gurus. Here Rinpoche tells the story of how Dharma came to Tibet, and how the eight practice lineages were formed.

The point of this exercise is given in the closing verses: history has brought the enlightenment legacy of the eight traditions into our time and world; we should access them and achieve enlightenment. The holder of them for us is our own guru, here seen in the form of Jamyang Khyentse Wangpo.

The liturgy of the fourth mindfulness of guruyoga — mindfulness of the enlightenment activities of the gurus — brings another presentation of the eight lineages. Here they are mentioned by name for the first time, rather than just being represented by their listed lineage masters, as was previously done. Again, Rinpoche has provided informative notes, and these have usually been incorporated into the text in brackets in my translation.

The liturgy of the fifth mindfulness — that of the transforming powers and blessings of the gurus — lists the principal doctrines of each of the eight, for it is these doctrines that infuse them with blessings and transformative powers.

The final mention of the eight comes in the concluding verses of spiritual aspiration. Here Rinpoche dedicates a verse to each of the eight (with the exception of two schools, that have to share one verse), in which a prayer is offered for the realizations of the wisdom teachings of each tradition. Here he skillfully weaves in the unique manner by which each school expresses the enlightenment experience, concluding with the aspiration that this be attained. As with the other sections in which the eight lineages are mentioned, here too there are lead-in and subsequent verses to the lineages from various perspectives.

Rinpoche's lead-in verses speak of a fourfold grouping of the eight: the middle view that balances the emptiness of ultimate reality with the conventional reality of illusory appearances, in which the laws of cause and effect operate; the path of mahamudra meditation, in which the naturalness of things is the focus of practice; cultivation of the experience of "one-tasteness" in all activity, in which happy and sad become one, pleasure and pain become one, and all experiences are made to arise as dharamakaya; and, finally, the resultant dzogchen, or great perfection. Rinpoche gives a verse to each of the four.

This portrays a vision of the Rimey approach to the wisdom trainings, and reveals the Rimey perspective on how the wisdom teachings of the eight traditions are brought into a single training regime. The formula is the fourfold application known as "view, meditation, activity and result." The view is madhyamaka, the meditation is mahamudra, the conduct is onetasteness, and the result is dzogchen.

Rinpoche blends many ideas and themes into his text. Its structure interweaves numerous themes: the six mindfulnesses of guruyoga; the seven-limbed devotion — prostrations, making offerings, acknowledging failings, rejoicing in goodness, requesting the gurus to turn the Dharma Wheel, requesting the gurus to live for long, and the dedication of merit; the rites known as outer, inner, secret and suchness offerings; recitation of the guru mantras; the tsok tantric feast offering/celebration; the meditation on taking the four empowerments; the prayer for accomplishing the realizations of the path; and so forth.

In a sense, it provides a complete map to the practices and philosophy of the Rimey path, presented in the form of a devotional liturgy.

Dilgo Khyentse's text is intended as a practice manual for chanting. It can be lengthened or shortened in various ways, described by Rinpoche himself in his chen, or "textual annotations," most of which I have included in parentheses. It can be adapted for use as a daily guruyoga practice, in which case it is abbreviated to roughly half its present length. Alternatively, Zhechen Monastery often uses it for a full-day tantric feast (Skt., ganachakra; Tib. tsok); when this is done, large sections of it are repeated several times, again as indicated by the author in his textual annotations.

I am delighted to have had the good karma to render Dilgo Khyentse Rinpoche's text into English, and ask the buddhas and bodhisattvas for their patience with any mistakes in the work. I had the great good fortune to meet Rinpoche several times during the 1970s and 1980s, and was deeply impressed by him. I also had the good fortune to receive a number of transmissions from him during those years, first in Bodh Gaya, and later in Tashi Jong and Dharamsala.

Of course one can never repay the kindness of the enlightenment masters. Nonetheless, I dedicate this small work to just that, and to the fulfillment of the visions and ideals of the sublime Rimey tradition.

The Structure of the Text

1. **Preparing the Place of Practice**

   (A) Invocation

   (B) Introductory Instructions

2. **The Preliminaries**

   (A) The preparations; and

   (B) The actual preliminaries

      1. Refuge and bodhichitta

      2. Expelling negative energies

      3. Consecration of the practice place and substances being used

3. **The Actual Practice**

   (A) First of the six mindfulnesses: Meditating on the Guru's Sublime Physical Presence

      1. The visualization for a simple individual practice

      2. Extending the Practice for Group Chanting

         a. The offering of bathing waters, etc.

         b. The seven-limbed offering to the Assembly of Rimey Masters

            i. Prostrations

            ii. Outer, inner, secret and suchness offerings

               a. Outer Offerings

                  • The general outer offerings

   (B) Second of the six mindfulnesses: Meditation on the Guru's Realizations

                  • Offering of all unowned things

(C) Third of the six mindfulnesses: Meditation on the Liberation Lives of the Gurus

        b. The Inner Offering, structured as a Vajrayogini *Tsok*

           • The Vajrayogini *Tsok*

           • The tantric offerings of the five sensory delights, etc.

(D) Fourth of the six mindfulnesses: Meditation on the Guru's Enlightenment Activity

        c. The secret offering

(E) Fifth of the six mindfulnesses: Meditating on the Transforming Powers (Blessings) of the Gurus

        d. The offering of suchness

(F) Sixth of the six mindfulnesses: Meditating on the Kindness (i.e., many benefits received from) the Gurus

        iii. Acknowledging one's faults

        iv. The remaining four limbs (of the seven limbed offering)

An offering of one's spiritual aspirations

    1. A general prayer to the Rimey Masters

    2. In particular, a prayer to the Nyingma Masters

Secondly, invoking the attention of the gurus through recitation of the name mantra

    1. The name mantra of Jamyang Khyentse Wangpo

    2. A general name mantra for all gurus

Thirdly, making requests for the fulfillment of aspirations and needs

4. The Concluding Activities

    (A) The tantric feast (*tsok*)

    (B) The thanksgiving offering

    (C) Taking the four tantric empowerments

        1. The vase empowerments

        2. The secret empowerment

        3. The wisdom empowerment

        4. The empowerment of the sacred instruction

    (D) The yoga of absorption

    (E) A concluding prayer

    (F) Concluding song of auspiciousness

Instructions on Adapting the Text for Personal Use

1. A note on abbreviating or expanding the ritual
2. A note on replacing Khyentse Wangpo with the Fifth Dalai Lama as the central image in the assembly visualized Rimey gurus
3. A note on replacing Khyentse Wangpo with one's own guru in the form of Vajrasattva and consort as the central image in the assembly visualized Rimey gurus

RIMEY LAMA CHOPA

A Tibetan Rimey Tantric Feast
A Rite to Invoke the Supreme Nectar of Wisdom

by Dilgo Khyentsey Rinpoche

Herein, arranged as a structured liturgy with the traditional stages of culti-vating inner aspirations and offering devotion, lies a practice of mindfulness focusing on the supreme non-affiliated masters in the Buddhist tradition.

Namo Guru Buddha Yah!

[Begin by stirring your mindstream with (general Mahayana) meditations such as those on spiritual detachment, coupled with the precious bodhichitta.

Cultivating the appropriate attitude toward one's spiritual teacher and engaging in profound single-pointed meditation focusing upon guruyoga is quintessential to success on the tantric path, the way of great mysteries whereby enlightenment is quickly achieved.

Along these lines, the Kadampa master Geshey Sharawa taught that we should cultivate the six mindfulnesses in our method of meditating on and contemplating the guru.

The meditation session, which integrates these six, is conducted in three phases: (1) the preliminaries; (2) the actual body of the method; and (3) the concluding phase.]

The Preliminaries

The preliminaries are twofold:
(A) the preparations; and (B) the actual preliminaries.

(A) The Preparations

[If the context of the practice session is that the day is a special occasion, such as a great celebration/commemoration in honor of the guru, begin by cleaning and refreshing the temple room. Arrange a platform in front of the altar, and cover it with a piece of good cloth. Next create an image of an eight-petalled lotus (on the cloth), either by sprinkling colored powders (i.e., sands) or else by conventional drawing or painting.

If this cannot be done, prepare a table or platform, anointing this with sweet scents. Place a mandala base on it, with nine mounds of grain, or a *menzi* (i.e., ritual bowl filled with grains). To symbolize the guru's presence, place an image of him, or a relic (such as a statue or reliquary amulet box containing things) such as fragments of hair or fingernails. Surround this with rows of offering bowls, however many hundreds or even thousands are being used.

The above is only done when the practice is being performed on a special occasion. For the yogi who performs the meditation on a more frequent basis, simply visualizing that the above has been done will suffice.]

(B) The Actual Preliminaries

Living beings, myself and others, vast in number as the measure of
    space,
Seek freedom from the ocean of samsaric imperfections,
Turn for inspiration to the Buddhas, Dharma and Sangha
And arouse the mind of compassionate bodhichitta
To meditate on the profound yoga.

[Recite this verse three times, or as much as is needed in order to arouse the appropriate mind state.]

[Now, if the occasion is such that the focus (of the gathering) is primarily a gurupuja celebration, the rite for expelling negative energies should be performed. This is done with the following words: —]

> I myself instantly appear (from emptiness)
> In the form of glorious Heruka Barwa Chenpo,
> The Great Blazing Fury.

> Whatever forces there are of negative predisposition,
> Be they gods, anti-gods, stalking spirits or just plain ghosts,
> All sources of negative energy wherever you are,
> Abiding in the pathways of body, speech and mind,
> I call to you; heed my words.

> I, Glorious Diamond Strength,
> Now establish the sacred wheel of protection;
> The radiant vajra blaze of my physical presence
> Easily subdues all negative forces.
> Spirit beings, I warn you, should you transgress me
> I will crush you; there is no other way.

[Recite the *Om sumbhani* mantra once, and then the following verse: —]

> Multicolored lights emanate out and then melt back.
> The Blazing Vajra Canopy, Dorje Barwaigur,
> Flashes a blaze of wisdom lights into all the directions
> And establishes the sacred protection wheel.
> Om vajra chakra raksha bhrum hum!

[This is the tantric way of meditating on establishing the wheel of protection.]

[Next follows the consecration of the practice place and substances being used. This begins with the mantra for purifying, and then the mantra for dissolving everything into emptiness: —]

Om vajra amrita kundali hana hana hum peh.
Om svabhava shuddho sarvadharma svabhava shuddho hoong.

Out of vast emptiness the mantric syllable BHRUM appears, and then transforms into a tantric mandala mansion made from precious jewels, complete with all characteristics. At its center, from syllables of OM, appear vessels made from precious jewels, vast and enormous, with a syllable of HUM inside each. These melt into light/nectar, and become the individual divine offerings, such as water for refreshing the mouth, water for cooling the feet, flowers, incense, light, herbal oils, ambrosial foods, music, the five sense-objects, the seven royal companions, the eight auspicious substances and also signs, and so forth. All these things appear in vessels held up by sixteen divine offering maidens.

These clouds of outer, inner and secret offerings are in essential nature wisdom itself, but appear in the forms of blissful offerings. They fill all of the skies, and have the nature of pouring forth incessantly for as long as samsara endures.

Om sarva bida pura pura sura sura avartaya hum svaha.

[Do the offering with the mantra: —]

Om vajra argham ah hum [...etc., until] shabte.

[Then the offering-cloud mantra: —]

Namo ratna tra ya ya. Om namo bhagawati vajra sara pramardane
tathagata ye arhate samyak sambuddha ya tadyata om vajra mahavajra

mahavidya vajra mahabodhichitta vajra mahabodhi mandopa samkara mana vajra sarva avarana bishodhana vajra sucha.

[Finally, with music, the blessing mantra: —]

Om vajra dharma ranita, praranita, samparauranita, sarva buddha kshetra, prachaliti, prajna paramita nada svabhave vajra dharma hrihdaya, santoshani hum hum hum hoh hoh hoh ah kham svaha.

[This completes the preliminaries. Now follows the actual practice.]

The Actual Practice

[The actual practice is comprised of the six mindfulnesses of the guru's presence. The first of these is that of recollecting the guru's physical presence. Therefore the first stage of the guruyoga meditation is the visualization of the assembly of holy beings, and offering devotion to them.]

Om shunyata jnana vajra svabhava atma ko ham.

Places and beings, mind and objects, are emptiness.
The singular, profound, non-duality wisdom emanates,
And without losing balance in the unity of physical and
    spiritual realities,
Reveals the world as a wondrous place,
A mysterious tantric paradise beneath none.

Before me, in the center of a mandala palace,
Amid enchanting clouds of offering jewels,
Seated on a throne upheld by eight lions,
On saffron cushions fashioned from beautiful brocades,
Is the all-encompassing Vajra Master, lord of the three mysteries,
Jamyang Khyentse Wangpo, emanation of Manjushri.

His hue is white tinged with red,
He is radiant with a marvelous glory,
His face is magnificent, and his eyes are opened wide.
His right hand holds a vajra,
His fingers in the mudra of abundance
(Holding the stem of a lotus on which sits) a life vase,
For he brings supreme spiritual knowledge
To fortunate trainees who apply themselves well.

His left is in the meditation mudra, and holds
A wisdom bell, as well as (the stem of) a lotus
On which sits a sacred scripture;
Thus he sits as he reveals the way of limitless Dharma.

He is clothed in the three Dharma robes
And wears the hat of a holder of the vast pitakas.
His feet are crossed in the vajra posture,
And he is seated with back erect.
In essence he is all Three Jewels collected as one,
An ocean-like embodiment of the Three Roots,
The three kayas inseparable,
A chakravartin master of the hundred buddha families,
In nature all spiritual forces brought together,
Merely a thought of whom drains the power of darkness,
Master aglow with every excellence and splendor.

[If the process of generating the visualized assembly is to be done in brief, the following liturgy can be used: —]

I request the masters of the lineages to come forth:
Nagarjuna and Asanga, the two chariots of India,
As well as the six ornaments of the world, and
Shantarakshita, Serlingpa, Jowo Jey Atisha,
Shakya Shri, the eighty-four mahasiddhas,
The three great Dharma kings,
The Abbot, Acharya and Entourage,
The masters of Tibet's ten great Dharma teaching lineages,
The masters of Tibet's eight great Dharma practice lineages,
The assembly of exalted masters of knowledge and practice,
Embodiments of the Three Jewels and Three Roots.
Perform the dance of unceasing wisdom
For the benefit of the trainees to be trained.
Come forth, and fill all the skies with your presence.

[Alternatively, if you have time for a more detailed visualization practice, this can be done with the following liturgy: —]

Above the crown of the glorious protector who encompasses all buddha families, the fearless all-accomplishing Jamgon Lama, the glorious Khyentse Wangpo, there suddenly appears a rainbow ball of light sending radiance into all directions.

Seated inside this vast radiance is the mighty guru Padma Sambhava Nangsi Zilnon, embodiment of the great wisdom of the buddhas of all times and ten directions, the Three Roots in one form.

His face is white tinged with red, and bears a wrathful smile. His body is adorned with the marks and signs of perfection, and blazes with supreme radiance.

Of his two hands, the right bears a golden five-pronged vajra held up toward the sky, with the fingers in the threatening mudra. His left is in the meditation gesture, and holds a skull cup bearing a life vase filled with the nectar of wisdom. A katvanga staff rests on his left shoulder.

His inner vest is of the white cloth symbolizing the secret tantric path, over which is a full-length blue tantric robe. Over these are the three orange Dharma robes, with a brocade cloak in red, the color of power. His head is adorned with a *sheu nyenzhu* hat, his two feet are in the royal posture, and he is seated on a lion throne, lotus and moon.

A great blaze of light from his body reveals his ubiquitous emanations, all of whom are inseparably one with him: the five families of skull-rosary gurus, the twelve knowledge holders, the eight emanation gurus, the thirteen wish-fulfilling jewel gurus, the six gurus who tame the living beings of the six realms, the forty-five illusory emanations, the hundred aspects, and so forth. These float in the halo that surrounds him, like dust floating in a ray of sunlight.

To his right, his mind at one with that of the great guru, is Vairochana Lotsawa, an all-illuminating sun of Dharma in Tibet. To his left is Trisong Deutsen, incarnation of Youthful Manjushri, who brought the roots and branches of Dharma to the Land of Snow Mountains. In front of him is the wisdom dakini Consort Yeshe Tsogyal of Kharchen, holder of secret

knowledge, incarnation of Sarasvati. They are surrounded by an ocean of
lotsawas, pandits, mahasiddhas and vidyadharas.

A wave of light emanates from the crown of the great guru. It manifests a host of lineage gurus, including Acharaya Vimalamitra, who achieved
the great transference to clear light; the accomplished Jnanasatra; the
vidyadhara Shri Singha; Acharya Manjushrimitra; the nirmanakaya master
Garab Dorje together with the twelve dzogchen revealers; the samboghakaya
peaceful and wrathful emanated tathagatas; and the dharmakaya Samantabhadra. These masters of the perfect play of the four visions, holders of the
three types of transmission — mind to mind, by signs, and by listening —
sit like flowers arranged delightfully around him.

Lights of five colors emanate forth from the life vase in the lotus to the
right of the Jamgon Lama (Khyentse Wangpo), the stem of which he holds
in the fingers of his right hand.

These flow out to the myriad of vajra realms, and reveal the glorious
mandala of the Wisdom Heruka, the mere thought of which arouses
supreme and common siddhis.

Seated within this pure sphere is the dharmakaya Buddha Vajradhara,
lord of all buddha families, revealer of the ocean of secret tantric teachings. His body is the color of lapis luzuli, and he is adorned with the robes
and ornaments of a samboghakaya emanation. His two hands hold a vajra
and bell at his heart, his feet are crossed in the vajra posture, and he is
seated on a lion throne, lotus and moon. He is surrounded by a gathering
of holders of the oceanic treasury of mysteries, such as Arya Lokeshvara
and Vajragarbha, Lord of the Ten Stages, as well as a myriad of dakas and
dakinis.

Also seated there are the (Indian) masters who received the transmissions of the four classes of secret tantras, including the lord of yogis
and mahasiddhas Saraha, Tilopa Prajnabhadra, Naropa Jnanasingha,
Vajra Krishnacharya, the mahasiddha Luhipa, the venerable Virupa, Vajra
Ghantapada, and all the principal figures from among the eighty-four
mahasiddhas. They shine with the glow of the great bliss accomplished by
means of vajra practice, and the radiance of their wisdom manifests the
mandala of Glorious Heruka, a mere thought of which bestows supreme

and common siddhis.

In the lotus beside the Jamgon Lama Khyentse Wangpo's left shoulder, the stem of which he holds in his left hand, are a sacred scripture and a wisdom sword. A rosary of rainbow lights emanates forth from these, and fills everything in samsara and nirvana.

It reveals the lord of Dharma, the incomparable Buddha Shakyamuni.

He is in his supreme nirmanakaya aspect, is adorned with the marks and signs of perfection, and is wearing the three Dharma robes. His right hand is in the earth-as-witness gesture, and his left, which bears his alms bowl, is in the gesture of meditation. With legs crossed in the vajra posture, he sits on a jewelled throne, lotus and moon. An assembly of Hinayana and Mahayana aryas surround him, including the eight close bodhisattva-disciples, such as Maitreya and Manjushri, the seven appointed successors, the sixteen arhats, and so forth.

Also seated around him are the various masters of his lineages of transmission, including Nagarjuna, chariot of the profound teachings on emptiness, together with his disciples; Asanga, clarifier of the vast bodhisattva way teachings, together with his brother Vasubhandu; the great bodhisattva Shantideva; the Indonesian master Serlingpa Dharmakirti; the second buddha Shantarakshita; the Kashmiri master Shakya Shri, who will manifest as a buddha of the future; and so forth.

In brief, all the great chariots who upheld and transmitted the pitakas, including the six ornaments and two supreme masters from India, and the six great doorkeepers, are seated around him like a golden rosary of mountains around Mount Meru, all of them ablaze with radiance and glory, like great lamps illuminating the three worlds.

To the right of Jamgon Lama (Khyentse Wangpo), king of Dharma, is the great transmitter of the bodhisattva teachings, source of millions of doctrine holders, Jowo Jey Atisha Dipamkara Shrijnana, together with the great translators who worked with him to open the Dharma path in Tibet, and the all-compassionate Sakya lamas who served as lords of the secret tantras.

To his left is the great chariot of the glorious Shangpa Kargyupa lineage, the illustrious Tangtong Gyalpo; Padampa Sanggye, who transmitted the supreme Zhijey Dharma lineage that pacifies all suffering; and Buton Rinchen Drup, the great chariot of the secret tantric teachings, through whom came the glorious Kalachakra lineages.

In front (of the Jamgon Lama, Khyentse Wangpo), in the center, is the king of treasure text revealers, Orgyen Terdak Lingpa, embodiment of all lineages; to his right is Jamgon Lodro Tayey (Jamgon Kongtrul the Great); to his left is the great treasure text revealer Chokgyur Lingpa; in front is Mipam Mawai Senge, as well as Jamyang Khyentse Chokyi Lodro, and the lord of all buddha families, Omniscient Longchen Rabjampa.

In the right corner is the great master of the *Mahamaya Tantra*, the lord of mysteries Zurchen Shakya Jungney; Sakya Pandita, transmitter of Dharma teachings; the lord of yogis, Jetsun Milarepa; and the great master of all Dharma lineages, the second buddha Tsongkhapa Lobzang Drakpa.

Off to the left is the illustrious grandfather lord of the ocean of treasure texts, Nyang Nyima Ozer; the great transmitter of the sutras and tantras combined, Panchen Padma Wanggyal; the Great Fifth Dalai Lama, Ngawang Lobzang Gyatso, a master of every Buddhist teaching; and the illustrious Gyalwang Karmapa Rangjung Dorje. Each of these figures is surrounded by their principal disciples, thus constituting vast a assembly beyond number.

Surrounding the group is a gathering of supreme masters: the gurus of the general Buddhist teachings, the gurus who lead disciples in the Dharma, the gurus who rejuvenate the Dharma in times of weakness, the gurus who transmit the oral tradition teachings, the gurus who arouse liberation in the mindstreams of disciples, and the gurus who perform the three acts of kindness.

In front of them are the mandala deities of the six classes of tantras; to their right are the supreme nirmanakaya emanations of the buddhas; behind them are stacks of holy scriptures embodying the Dharma teachings; and to the right are the Hinayana and Mahayana sangha. Between them are the myriads of dakas, dakinis, Dharma protectors, wealth gods, and spirits that reveal treasures. These are so numerous that they fill the skies, like thick rain-clouds in summer.

All of these holy beings embody mastery of the various spiritual natures, and manifest an illusory net of incessantly playful wisdom dramas of body, speech, mind and activity in order to train those to be trained. Their physical presences shine brightly with the outer, inner and secret signs of accomplishment. The melodious sounds of their voices open countless Dharma doors. Their minds blaze with the lights of compassion, wisdom and power. Their realizations and enlightenment activities spontaneously accomplish their goals.

At the crown of the great guru is a white syllable OM, at his throat is a red AH, and at his heart is a blue HUM. These emanate great waves of light, that summon forth from the vast pure realms the various aspects of the three kayas, such as the gurus and buddhas, together with their disciples.

Vajra samaya jah.

[Having recited the above liturgy, generate the conviction that this vast assembly of visualized gurus actually manifests, and that they are present in the space in front of you. Meditate with mindfulness for an extended period of time on their physical presence. Doing this, together with an offering of a prayer to them for blessings, is sufficient on occasions of individual practice.

When the practice is done by a large gathering as part of a gurupuja celebration, then it is good to perform an invocation (such as is described in the following) liturgy. Begin by offering incense, and then chant melodiously: —]

Spiritual forces of all times and directions,
Embodiments of the Three Jewels of Refuge,
Look with compassion on the deluded living beings;
Emanate magically and without hindrance
From the myriad pure realms; manifest here now
Amidst the ocean of cloud-like offerings.
Ratna guru sapariwara vajra samaya jah.

[Requested in this way, they come forth and manifest.]

Jah hum bam hoh. The invoked holy beings become inseparably one with the visualized forms.

[If the occasion is a large gathering, it is good here to chant the verses of offering bathing waters to the holy beings, drying their bodies, offering raiment, and so forth. The liturgies for these are not given here, but (as they are well-known to all practitioners) this should not be considered an oversight.]

[Secondly is the phase of accumulating spiritual energies. To do this in an extensive way, one performs the seven-limbed devotion, together with the remaining five mindfulnesses. The first of these seven devotions is that of prostration: —]

In the space in front (of me) I envision the assembly of meritorious beings, and in their presence emanate forms of myself and others as numerous as the atoms of all worlds, which engage in the stages of merit-gathering, such as offering prostrations.

> With my palms pressed together above the crown of my head,
> My fingers together like the petals of a flower bud,
> Like upstretched petals of a young lotus in a beautiful pool,
> I give melodious voice to these verses of prostration
> With my countless emanated forms.

> I offer homage at the feet of the all-kind masters,
> The incomparable gurus who are precious buddhas,
> And who embody the blessings of the body, speech and mind
> Of the tathagatas of the three times and their disciples.

> I offer homage to the gurus on whom fell the instructions:
> The primordial buddha Samantabhadra, the five tathagatas,
> The bodhisattvas of the three natures — compassion, wisdom and
>   power —

Garab Dorje, Shri Singha, and Gyalpo Dza, master of all five buddha
    families;
And to the eight supreme holders of Buddha's secret teachings.

I offer homage to all the gurus of the transmission lineages
Who mastered the well-spoken teachings of the Buddha
And the commentaries of the later Buddhist masters,
Such as the pratimoksha, bodhisattva and tantric precepts,
And the three pitakas of vinaya, sutra and abhidharma.

I offer homage to the gurus who transmitted the ocean-like teachings
Of the nine vehicles of the vast and profound Dharma:
Masters of the shravaka, pratyekabuddha and bodhisattva ways,
And of the tantric paths known as kriya, charya, yoga, mahayoga, anu
    and ati.

I offer homage to the past masters of incomparable kindness:
Padma Sambhava, embodiment of all buddhas,
And his disciples such as Vimala;
And to Shantarakshita, the sun illuminating Dharma in Tibet,
And the three Dharma kings, especially Trisong Deutsen.

I offer homage to the lineages of instruction and treasure gurus:
To the twenty-five close disciples; and to
So and Zur, [transmitters of the mahayoga tantras, especially
    "The Illusory Display"], Noob, [transmitter of the anuyoga
    tantras, especially "The Gathering of the Great Assembly,"]
And Nyang, [revealer of profound treasures];
And to the line of pandits, scholars and adepts,
As well as the emanation masters who revealed the great
    treasure texts.

I offer homage to the countless mahasiddhas:
Indrabuthi [transmitter of the male tantra Guhyasamaja],

Virupa [transmitter of the female tantra Hevajra],

Saraha [transmitter of mahamudra and the Buddhakapali Tantra],

Luhipa, Krishnacharya and Ghantapada [transmitters of the Heruka
    Chakrasamvara Tantra],

Buddhaguhya [transmitter of the kriya, charya and yoga tantras],

Lilavajra [master of the non-dual Kalachakra],

Kalachakrapada [also known as Chilupa, who was Directly blessed by
    the Shambhala masters],

And all the Indian mahasiddhas who contributed to the dissemination
    of the tantric teachings.

I offer homage to the supreme jewels of India:

Nagarjuna [who was blessed by Manjushri and who

So wonderfully articulated the profound teachings on emptiness],

Together with his chief disciple Aryadeva,

Asanga [who was blessed by Maitreya and who taught the vast
    bodhisattva ways],

His brother [Vasubandhu, who compiled the abhidharma teachings],

Dignaga and Dharmakirti [compilers of the pramana doctrines],

Acharya Dharmapala [elucidator of the middle view],

Gunaprabha and Shakyaprabha [the two great vinaya masters],

And the wondrous poet Acharya Vira.

I offer homage to the founders of the ten teaching lineages:

Tonmi Sambhota [Tibet's first real translator],

Bero [translator of the three pitakas and four tantra classes],

Ka, Chok, Zhang and Palgyi Dorje,

Rinchen Zangpo and Ngok Lotsawa [who initiated the new schools],

Sakya Panchen [who mastered the sutras, tantras and ten branches of
    knowledge],

Buton Rinchen Drubpa [great compiler of vinaya, abhidharma,
    prajnaparamita, pramana and tantric teachings],

And the other illustrious gurus in the lineage.

I offer homage to Jowo Atisha Dipamkara, lord of the bodhichitta
    teachings,
The venerable Sakyapa, a fountain of secret tantras,
The Kargyupa masters, incomparable practitioners of the golden path,
And the holders of the Shangpa "Golden Dharmas."

I offer homage to the masters of the eight practice lineages,
Such as Tsongkhapa, the lion's roar of transmissions and reason,
The masters of the Zhijey tradition, who use sutra and tantra in union,
The masters of the Kalachakra Tantra transmission,
And the Nyendrup masters, who composed
Hundreds of guides to the various tantric retreat methods.

I offer homage to all masters who uphold the Dharma
By teaching the path, guiding disciples, giving initiations,
Reviving the Dharma in times of weakening,
Imparting oral instructions, liberating the minds of trainees,
And engaging in teaching, practice and Dharma work.

I offer homage to all spiritual forces of all times and directions:
The incomparable Three Jewels of Refuge,
The mandala deities, dakas and dakinis of the six classes of tantras,
And the Dharmapalas, wealth deities and treasure gods.

I offer homage to all objects worthy of this respect,
My mind absorbed in the sphere of spiritual devotion,
And visualizing that my bodily forms are as numerous
As the number of atoms found in all world systems.
Om guru sarva tathagata kaya vaka chitta pranamen
    bhandhanam karomi.

[Secondly is the limb of offering. Here the substances should be understood
as being in nature the realizations of the path, and that these have taken the
form of the outer offerings.]

This water of eight excellences able to induce detachment,
In nature a happy stream of pure pratimoksha discipline
Quencher of thirst, a delight to all divine beings,
I offer to the assembly of gurus, embodiments of all the buddhas.
Om ratna guru sapariwara vajra argham puja megha samudra
saparana samaye hum.

This sweetly fragrant water of teachings beneficial to all,
That washes away the hundred stains of selfishness,
Cooling water that fulfills the purposes of living beings
Who practice the path of self-discipline,
I offer to the assembly of gurus, embodiments of all the buddhas.
Om ratna guru sapariwara vajra padyam puja megha samudra
saparana samaye hum.

Pure wisdom manifest as form, stunning in beautiful colors,
Rich in nectar that delights all living beings equally,
A flower garden with a wisdom dance of radiance and drama,
I offer to the assembly of gurus, embodiments of all the buddhas.
Om ratna guru sapariwara vajra pushpe puja megha samudra
saparana samaye hum.

A cloud of incense with the sweet fragrance of devotion
Able to pervade to the radiant mind
And inspire the heart in the practice of the path,
I offer to the assembly of gurus, embodiments of all the buddhas.
Om ratna guru sapariwara vajra dhupe puja megha samudra
saparana samaye hum.

This lamp of wisdom able to dispel dark ignorance,
That illuminates reality with a thousand light-rays
And brings delight to all awakened beings,
I offer to the assembly of gurus, embodiments of all the buddhas.

Om ratna guru sapariwara vajra aloke puja megha samudra
   saparana samaye hum.

This ocean of herbal oils able to heal every ill
And restore the vitality of youthful splendor,
A delight to the touch, cool and fragrant,
The mere sight of which furthers harmony in the world,
I offer to the assembly of gurus, embodiments of all the buddhas.
Om ratna guru sapariwara vajra gandhe puja megha samudra
   saparana samaye hum.

This ambrosial food of a hundred wondrous flavors
In a vast jewelled vessel, symbol of the generous mind,
The taste of which fulfills all spiritual and worldly needs,
I offer to the assembly of gurus, embodiments of all the buddhas.
Om ratna guru sapariwara vajra naividya puja megha samudra
   saparana samaye hum.

Pure music complete with seven limbs of melody,
A million notes of melodious teachings of the Three Ways,
The mere sound of which brings freedom from samsara and nirvana
I offer to the assembly of gurus, embodiments of all the buddhas.
Om ratna guru sapariwara vajra shabte puja megha samudra
   saparana samaye hum.

[If this offering is to be done in an abbreviated form: —]

In order to delight Jamgon Khyentse Wangpo, master of all spiritual
   natures,
I offer the glorious seven precious jewels;
In form outer offerings, in essence they are the seven inner gems.
Please accept them, and bestow waves of inspiring blessings.
Om ratna guru sapariwara vajra argham (and so forth, until
   shabte) puja megha samudra.

[Secondly, mindfulness of the guru's realizations: —]

From the deep and silent sphere of the uncontrived essence,
The utter simplicity of dharmakaya clear light,
The realm of the primordial buddha Samantabhadra,
Comes a cloud of peaceful and wrathful deities,
Samboghakaya forms of the five buddha families, with
The blissful wisdom of five qualities and seven natures.

Then, born from the power of great compassion,
Countless nirmanakaya emanations fill the skies,
Such as Shakyamuni Buddha, who taught the Dharma in India,
And Guru Padma Sambhava, who brought Dharma to Tibet;
They work to bring benefit to the beings to be trained, and
To further joy and goodness in the world.

The precious spiritual masters and jewel-like gurus
Are inseparably one with the dharmakaya of all buddhas.
In teaching the Dharma and working for the world,
They are indistinguishable from the tathagatas themselves,
Measureless in wisdom, compassion and power.

It is through the kindness of the compassionate gurus
That we enter into the enlightenment path
And are guided to spiritual realization.
Fearless in the practice of the three higher trainings,
They embody every quality of learning and insight.

The merit of making a small offering to a single pore of the guru
Of the light of a butterlamp with a single drop of oil
Excels that of making countless offerings over many aeons
To all the buddhas of the three times and ten directions.
Thus his kindness is beyond all reckoning.

O Jamyang Khyentse Wangpo, lord of knowledge and compassion,
You and all of the great Rimey masters of the past
In secret essence were actually Buddha Vajradhara
Manifest as adepts, yogis, translators and pandits
In order to train the beings to be trained.
Merely by offering a heartfelt prayer to you,
All empowerments, blessings and siddhis are acquired.
Your qualities of transcendence and realization
Are as measureless as the sky and the oceans,
And your works in training the beings to be trained
Surpass all fantasies.

[Contemplate the meaning of these verses on the excellence of the spiritual masters, until an actual feeling for the vastness of their kindness arises.]

[Secondly, the offering of all unowned things: —]

In the pure realm of the space-pervading bodhichitta
The qualities of the aryas manifest as mountains, lands and seas.
This world which delights the buddhas and bodhisattvas
I offer to the guru, who has accomplished the two goals.

[The practice can be done in brief in this way. Otherwise, if a longer liturgy is required, the following can be used: —]

On the mandala offering base made of the four elements
Symbolizing the four immeasurable mind-states,
I place the five strengths and five powers
As Mount Meru and the four continents
The seas between the continents being
The four transcendences and four mindfulnesses.
This abundant world of enlightenment qualities
I offer to the all-kind guru.

The precious mountains and rocks are generosity and discipline;
The forests adorned with herbs are patience and joyous energy;
The lakes and gardens are meditation and wisdom.
This abundant world reflecting the six perfections
I offer to the all-kind guru.

The vast space of the perfection of skillful wisdom
Is embellished with the sun, moon and stars that are
The perfection of spiritual aspiration;
Rainbows, rain clouds and thunder are the perfection of the
    ten strengths,
And the rain that falls is primordial awareness itself.
This abundant world reflecting all spiritual qualities
I offer to the all-kind guru.

The world of form is the seven limbs of enlightenment,
The eight auspicious emblems are the noble eightfold path,
The eight auspicious substances are the forces of
Freedom, wisdom's power and clairvoyance.
These abundant riches of the enlightened beings
I offer to the all-kind guru.

The visualized precious gems are the ten arya stages,
Jewels and ornaments are the five paths to enlightenment;
In the spirit of celebration I offer these spiritual riches
Pleasing to gods, nagas and humans alike.
O assembly of glorious gurus, accept them with delight.

[This offering is stylized to reflect the essence of the meaning of the Sutra-yana teachings. As you engage in the practice, imagine that you and all other living beings give rise in your mindstream to the actual experience of the stages of transcendence and insight embodied in the text.]

[Thirdly, cultivating mindfulness of the liberating lives of the great gurus: —]

Out of compassion, the Buddha offered five hundred prayers
To be able to benefit this world filled with conflict,
And was praised for being like a white lotus
[That grows beautiful and unstained in a muddy pool].
For ages the compassionate master strove tirelessly
Without concern for body and life
To gather the treasures of Dharma knowledge,
Enduring great hardships, like walking through fire,
Having his body pierced with nails,
And walked in his quest to achieve spiritual realization
Until his feet were ragged and worn.

The sutra and tantra paths that he taught
Are inseparable from his dharmakaya nature;
To study, teach, read or memorize writings of his words
Brings delight to the great bodhisattvas,
Such as Manjushri, Vajrapani and Maitreya,
And to the masters who were guided and blessed by them,
Such as the six ornaments and two supreme sages of India,
And the seven masters appointed by the Buddha.

It also delights the masters of the tantric path
Whose playful wisdom directly perceives reality itself,
Including Buddha Vajradhara and the treasury of wisdom dakas and
    dakinis,
The tantric lineage founders, such as Luhipa, Krishnacharya,
    Ghantapada, Saraha,
And all yogic masters who unmistakenly entered the doors of
    spiritual experience
And established the character of the enlightenment path
Through study, contemplation, meditation,
Discussion, debate and composition, cultivating the ways

Of learning, transcendence and sublime being,
And transmitting these for the benefit of future ages,
Thus becoming worthy of every respect.

Then as though the Buddha himself had come again,
The great guru Padma Sambhava appeared.
Assisted by Shantarakshita and King Trisong Deutsen,
He brought the sunlight of Dharma to Tibet.
Through the inconceivable deeds of these early masters
In transmitting the original teachings of the Buddha,
As well as the work of the treasure text revealers,
The darkness of the land was gradually dispelled.

And the great Indian guru Jowo Atisha appeared.
He gathered the lineages of countless masters
Who had attained the stages of profound realization,
Such as the Indonesian guru Lama Serlingpa Dharmakirti,
And after accomplishing their essence he came to Tibet,
Where he established the wondrous Kadam School.*

[*In which every instruction of the Buddha can be integrated for the
enlightenment of an individual practitioner; called "wondrous" because
texts, precepts and oral instructions are all brought into harmony.]

The essence of great compassion, the great Sakyapa Lama,
Who was blessed by (the Indian mahasiddha) Virupa,
Transmitted the ocean of secret tantric texts
Spread the complete teachings of the Buddha,
And established the wondrous Sakya School.

The master Marpa, with great personal hardship and danger,
Travelled to India and Nepal, where he
Studied with masters such as Naropa and Maitripa,
And through mastering the instructions of the pandits and adepts

Established a tradition of pure practice
That was transmitted through a number of lines
Collectively called the Kargyu, or "Instruction Lineage"*

[* This includes schools such as the Tropu, Drukpa, Tsalpa, Karma
Khamtsen, Drikung, Taklung, Yazang and Pakmo Drupa. All of these
combine the waters of two streams: that of Ka, which are the oral transmissions of the Kadam School (the Ka syllable having the same spelling in
both Kargyu and Kadam); with gyu, or "lineage," in this case the "lineage"
referring to the mahamudra transmission.]

Having trained under a hundred and fifty Indian masters
And acquired the close lineage that is the life-drops of the dakinis,
The lord of yogis Khyungpo Naljor, a master of the three worlds,
Established the Shangpa School, based on
The essence of five highest tantra teachings,*
Which passed through the great mahasiddha Tangtong Gyalpo.

[*These five include Chakrasamvara, which has the highest teaching
on karmamudra; Hevajra, which has the highest teaching on inner fire;
Guhyasamaja, with the highest teaching on clear light; Mahamaya, with the
highest teaching on the illusory body and dream yogas; and Vajrabhairava,
which has the highest teaching on tantric activity.]

Padampa Sanggyey, famed in both India and Tibet,
Drew from the lineages of fifty-four yogis and yoginis
And their sutra and tantra instructions;
He established the Zhijey School, which takes as its focus
The Tsar-chod method of ego-exorcism.*

[*Known as Zhijey, or "Pacifying," because ordinary Buddhist practice aims
at pacifying negative action and the distorted mind, whereas these yogas aim
at pacifying physical problems and illness. Chod uses the teachings of the
prajnaparamita sutras as its basis.]

The great non-dual quick path of Vajrasattva,
With Kalachakra [and its six completion-stage yogas],
Guhyasamaja [and its path of five stages],
Hevajra [with the Lam Drey "Path and Fruit" tradition],
And Samvara [with its three, four and five-pronged approaches],
Using tantric initiation to ripen study and practice,
Becomes the quick route of the generation [mahayoga]
And completion [anuyoga] stage yogas, coupled with
The sublime teaching of Dzogchen, the Great Perfection
[With the traditions of sem (mind), long (depth) and man-ngak (oral
    instruction)],
Having four knowledge holders, the early transmissions
And the great mysterious treasure texts,
Carrying seekers to the stage of vajra enlightenment
Through the four and six tantra classes.
Indeed inconceivable is the kindness of the lineage lamas
Who established and transmitted this extraordinary legacy.

The streams of all these different lineages
Were gathered by Jamyang Khyentse Wangpo,
Without weakening, mixing or mistaking any of them,
And were transmitted to disciples of quality and destiny.
The treasury of profound teachings emanating from this vast array of
    masters
Was also collected by Lodro Tayey (Jamgon Kongtrul), embodiment
    of Dharma's lifelines,
A wish-fulfilling jewel among Dharma lords.
Who is there today to equal them?

These Indian and Tibetan chariots, together with
The masters who followed in their lineages,
Were like the Buddha himself and the great bodhisattvas
In upholding and transmitting spiritual knowledge.
Those wishing liberation follow their way.

The illustrious and exalted spiritual masters
Themselves have transcended worldly concerns,
But out of great compassion and concern for the world
They remain in the world to increase the world's good.

Taking a bodily form like those of the beings to be trained,
They transcend all attachment to wealth, body and even life,
Ignore hundreds of hardships in their spiritual dedication,
And come to embody a secret treasury of spiritual knowledge.
Theirs' is the stage of vajra realization,
And receiving a single bead from their rosary of teachings
Brings quick and easy enlightenment.
Merely hearing the sound of their names is rare.

The quintessential nature of their teachings,
The extracted essence of all the sutras and tantras,
Passed over centuries through the generations of masters,
Is said to be a vast, profound diamond of unfailing transformations,
Fabulous and profound instructions for authentic practice
Made available through the great kindness of the guru.

[The above verses make references to the great masters of the past and their deeds, and to their role in collecting and transmitting the teachings. We should reflect on them, until the mind of strong spiritual conviction arises.]

[Secondly, the inner offering, which here is structured as a Vajrayogini *tsok* celebration : —]

> In front of me the syllable YAM instantly appears
> And becomes an air mandala; RAM becomes fire;
> Above that, KAM becomes a tripod of three human heads.
> My own mind, in nature Vajrayogini,
> Leaves my body via my brahma aperture.
>
> With the curved knife in her right hand,
> She slices off my head above my eyebrows;
> This skull-cup becomes huge and vast;
> My body is placed inside it
> And chopped into little pieces.
>
> Wind from the air mandala moves below,
> And the fire mandala is ignited;
> The substances in the skull cup melt and boil.
> All faults leave with the rising bubbles,
>
> And the steam emanates lights into all directions.
> This then draws back into the skull cup,
> Bringing with it the essence of all realizations,
> Which (appears in the skull) in the form of nectar.
>
> This offering cloud of mystical substances,
> The mere taste or touch of which induces non-samsaric bliss,
> Is scooped out in a ladle and then
> Offered to the objects of devotion.
>
> Light rays emanate from the tongues
> Of the vajra masters, embodiments of the Three Jewels,
> And drink the essence of this divine offering.
> "Please grant me siddhi."

Vajra rays emanate from the tongues
Of the peaceful and wrathful mandala deities
And drink of my offering.
"Please bestow transforming powers."

Weapon rays emanate from the tongues
Of the dakas, dakinis, dharmapalas and prosperity deities
And drink of my offering.
"Please dispel obstacles."
To this feast also are invited
The living beings of the six realms,
All of whom once were father and mother to me,
Including all good and evil gods, ghosts, and hindering spirits.

This nectar of my purified body I offer
To each and every one of you without exception.
May it become food, drink, clothing,
Or whatever it is that is needed.

May it inspire the universal love of bodhichitta,
Repay any karmic debts that are owed,
And cause omniscient buddhahood
To be quickly attained.

By any meritorious energy from my offering
This rite, in which the substances, vessel and implements
Are all by nature unapprehendable dharmakaya,
Emptiness pure from the beginning,
Three circles void of inherent being,
May myself, others and all living beings
Complete the two accumulations
And achieve the state of buddhahood
That is free from all obscurations.

[One should perform the according visualization and meditation while chanting the above lines.]

[Now follows the vajra sensory offering, together with the threefold offering known as "*men* (amrita), *rakta* and *torma*": —]

> I hold up an ocean of vajra sensory offerings
> And fill the vast dharmakaya skies with them:
> Form with the elegance of wisdom, melody free from ego,
> Scent which is in nature pure ethics,
> The taste of the four tantric pleasures,
> And touch which is the three types of mudras.

[If this is to be done in brief, the above liturgy will suffice. If it is to be done extensively, the liturgy below should be used: —]

> My skandhas and elements purified in the net of discipline,
> And the oath to give rise only to supreme great bliss, the best
>   of bodhichittas,
> Take form as the five amrita nectars.
> I offer this to the guru, lord of the mandala circle.
> The life prana released into the central channel,
> Divorced from conceptual ideas of mind and its objects, and
>   of all in the three worlds,
> Ordinary lust purified: this takes form as maharudhi.
> I offer this to the guru, lord of the mandala circle.
>
> The six aspects of the mind, both mind and its objects,
> All without exception melt into clear light
> And re-appear as a treasure for the senses,
> A maha balimta torma for tantric practice.
> I offer this to the guru, lord of the mandala circle.

[Fourthly, cultivating mindfulness of the guru's enlightenment activities: —]

The beings of this dark age, such as myself,
Obscured by karmic instincts and other distortions,
Have not the good fortune to meet with the Buddha
Nor to hear him teach the supreme Dharma.
The forces of our klesha are strong,
The power of the antidotes weak,
And we are poor when it comes to the wealth
Of spiritual conviction, joyous effort and wisdom.
In times such as this, to arouse
Even a small spiritual thought is rare.

But it is just as though the Buddha himself had come again;
For the gurus impart the oral tradition teachings
Which extract the essence of the sutras and tantras,
Are easily understood, quintessential,
And provide a fast path to buddhahood
For trainees of intelligence and good fortune.

The mind of the Buddha is beyond all faults,
And the intent of the sutra and tantra masters profound.
But the gurus who perform the enlightenment activity
Of leading trainees in accord with their needs
On the sublime path leading to buddhahood
Are praised as being more marvelously kind to us
Than any of the buddhas or early masters,
For it is they who come directly into our life.

This is true with chariots of all the schools:
The (Kadam and Geluk) Lam Rim tradition of three spiritual
    perspectives;
The (Sakya) "Three Visions Tradition" as preliminary
And Lam Drey doctrine of tantric application;

The (Kargyu) tradition on the nature of being [initiation],
Method [the six yogas of Naropa], freedom [mahamudra],
And the fruits of the path [yuganaddha, "the great union"];
The (Shangpa) legacy of root [the six yogas of Niguma],
Trunk [mahamudra], leaves [the three kayas as the path],
Flowers [the red and white Vajrayogini practices]
And fruit [undying/unmoving];
The (Zhijey) tradition of pacification
[Which integrates four blessings from the Buddha:
Tantric methodology, the view of the Prajnaparamita Sutras,
Great compassion, and the bodhisattva ethic],
And the Tsar Chod tradition ("Cutting the Root," or ego-exorcism,
    which integrates Prajnaparamita and Tantra),
Thus uniting the meaning of the sutras and tantras;
The Vajra Yoga (or Orgyen Nyendrup of the siddha Orgyenpa);
The Six Kalachakra yogic applications (of the Zhalu tradition);
And the (Nyingma) tradition of three inseparable vajras
And four yogic accomplishments, together with
Generation stage [mahayoga], completion stage [anuyoga]
And the Great Perfection [atiyoga].*

[*One should understand the code words used by the different traditions in accordance with the annotations provided in the lines above.

[If possible, at this point in the process one can pause from the liturgy and meditate on the individual teachings referred to. One should generate a strong sense that if one applies oneself to these various oral tradition teachings one will definitely be able to achieve the desired results in this very lifetime.]

[Thirdly, the secret offering: —]

> The wisdom experience of the four emptinesses,
> Aroused by means of the four tantric joys,
> Manifests as youthful maidens of great beauty,
> Who play stringed instruments, flutes, and various drums,
> Perform dramas, songs and dances,
> And present offerings of flowers, incense,
> Light, herbal oils, forms, touches and flavors.
> These delightful dharmadhatu mudras,
> Supreme messengers of the buddhas active in all ways,
> Are adorned with the sublime signs of the five natures,
> And merely thinking of them bestows the miracle
> Of the wisdom of bliss and emptiness.

[If this is done in brief, then the lines "The wisdom experience of the four emptinesses, aroused by means of the four tantric joys...," has the same meaning as the first line in the short liturgy, which is as follows: —]

> Sixteen fabulous vajra goddesses
> Dance into every direction with offerings.
> In the complete mandala of non-samsaric delight
> They pay homage to the body, speech and mind of the guru
> In order to bring constant pleasure and joy.

> Om bini vajrini ah hum.
> Om vamse vajrini ah hum.
> Om muranja vajrini ah hum.
> Om mira tamgi vajrini ah hum.
> Om lasya vajrini ah hum.
> Om hasya vajrini ah hum.
> Om girta vajrini ah hum.
> Om nirti vajrini ah hum.
> Om pushpe vajrini ah hum.

Om dhupe vajrini ah hum.
Om aloke vajrini ah hum.
Om gandhe vajrini ah hum.
Om rupa vajrini ah hum.
Om rasa vajrini ah hum.
Om parsha vajrini ah hum.
Om dharmadhatu vajrini ah hum.

[Fifthly, cultivating mindfulness of the guru's transforming powers: —]

Merely a glance from the compassionate mind of the guru
Sprouts the seeds of the path of liberation
In the streams of even ordinary beings;
This gives birth to the common spiritual qualities,
Such as detachment, clarity, joyous energy and wisdom.

The gurus link us to the uncommon ground
Of the vajra path of ripening and liberation;
And then their instructions on the generation and completion stage
    yogas
Bestow the two siddhis: those common and those supreme.

Especially, the great bliss of innate wisdom is aroused
In accord with the teachings of the gurus
Of the various sutra and tantra traditions:
The [Kadampa transmission] of the means for cultivating
The conventional and ultimate enlightenment minds;
The [Sakyapa transmission] of the inseparability
Of samsara and nirvana, and the flow of energies on the basis-of-all;
The [Kargyu transmission of] the innate clear light;
The [Shangpa doctrine] of primordial awareness mahamudra;
The [Zhijey transmission which] extracts the essence
Of the wisdom of the emptiness teachings
From the Mother Prajnaparamita Sutras;

The [Kalachakra doctrine] of the vajra mind, with
The supremely immutable wisdom of bliss and emptiness;
The [Dorje Nyendrubpa doctrine] of the subtle drop and the
    primordial mind;
And the [Nyingma doctrine] of the innate purity
That pervades everything in samsara and nirvana.

In their final meaning, all these legacies of instruction
Have one and the same taste, and the same essential message
Of how the ultimate nature of being is unfabricated,
And is omnipresent in all times and places.

O precious gurus, a mere moment of faith in you
Has the power to awaken the mind to this reality.
By relying upon the power of your blessing,
The warmth of the experience of the signs of progress
Naturally causes all spiritual realizations to grow,
Like grass under the warm summer skies.

The six perfections of the Sutrayana path blossom,
And the common and supreme siddhis
Of the Mantrayana Way are quickly achieved.

In brief, in a single moment the guru can arouse
The seeds of realization within a trainee,
Bringing the breath of new life to those
Suffocated by the constrictions of worldly existence.

Is not meeting with this legacy more rare
Than meeting with even the Buddha himself?
All of these marvelous effects arise
Solely through the inspiration of the gurus.
Through their waves of uplifting blessings,
All wishes are fulfilled and all paths accomplished.

Aware of this, I turn with joy and intense presence
And call to the gurus with a pressing voice:
Bestow your powerful blessing waves now
And reveal the wondrous tantric path to me.

[In brief, all the realizations of the paths leading to liberation and enlightenment arise solely from the blessings of the guru, and all obstacles to progress
are dispelled by reliance upon him. Understanding this, remain in mindfulness of the power of the guru's blessings.]

[Fourthly, the offering of suchness: —]

Myself and all the things I experience in life
Are mere unobstructed appearances,
Like the moon reflected in water.
If we look at these phenomena, they have no real being,
And in nature are emptiness free from the eight extremes.
From within this vision I make offerings to the guru.

All the objects that arouse attraction and desire in me —
Beautiful places, my body, things, the opposite sex, and family —
I dedicate to enlightenment and offer to the guru.
Accept them within the sphere of your playful humor
That abides in the all-distinguishing wisdom
And looks on all beings without attachment;
Facilitate my practice of the perfection of generosity.

All the objects that arouse anger and hatred within me —
Beings who show me enmity, harm me or speak with ugly and heavy
    words —
I dedicate to enlightenment and offer to the guru.
Accept them within the sphere of your ornament
That is the sublime mirror-like wisdom;
Release a nectar rain of love on all living beings.

All the objects that arouse pride and arrogance within me —
Family background, body, wealth, qualities and ideas —
I dedicate to enlightenment and offer to the guru.
Accept them within the sphere of your glory
Born from the wisdom that sees everything as equal;
And thus may all beings be propelled to the stage
Of the svabhavakaya, the natural essence of being.

All the objects that arouse jealousy and envy within me —
The successes and glories gained by other living beings —
I dedicate to enlightenment and offer to the guru.
Accept them within the sphere of your nature
That is one with the all-accomplishing wisdom;
May all beings achieve the splendors of enlightenment
And manifest the deeds of a buddha's nirmanakaya.

All the objects toward which I have ignorance or confusion,
Such as non-duality in the practice of
Transcending negativity and cultivating goodness,
I dedicate to enlightenment and offer to the guru.
Accept them within the sphere of your nature
That is one with the dharmadhatu wisdom;
May all beings gain realization of the dharmakaya state
That sees the one reality within all things equally.

The offering substances are in nature divine wisdom;
The merit field is the assembly of gurus.
I make this offering in clear appreciation
That from the very beginning my own mind
Has by nature been non-duality, and is free of self-nature,
Abiding as it does in the sphere of pure being.

[One should make this offering with awareness of the blissful wisdom that
realizes how everything is made equal in emptiness, and how the three

circles (of subject, object and interchange between them) are without any trace of duality. In this way one offers to the guru with appreciation of how all things in samsara and nirvana, including the practice of the spiritual path, that involves transcending faults and cultivating excellences, are without any true existence.]

[Sixthly, cultivating mindfulness of the kindness of (i.e. benefits received from) the guru: —]

> For those like me born in this dark age of conflict,
> Relying on the glory of the guru's compassionate guidance
> Brings great meaning to this precious human life,
> For it provides access to a secret treasury of tantric teachings
> That are difficult to acquire in even aeons of lifetimes.

> Relying on the kindness of the compassionate guru
> Brings the treasure of vast and profound Dharma jewels
> And lays the root for gaining the realizations of the path.
> Meeting the Buddha is rare, but even more so is the fortune
> Of meeting with the tantric path,
> Which has descended to us from Buddha Vajradhara
> And was established in Tibet by the eight great practice lineages.

> This precious Dharma, more wondrous than the most cherished of
>   gems,
> The very life-essence of the teachings of the Buddha,
> Was introduced by the ten great teaching lines,
> Disseminated by the generations of qualified masters,
> And through the kindness of the glorious protecting guru
> Becomes a resource available to us as individuals today.

> The direct teachings of the gurus are
> The essence of the sutras and tantras
> And the life-drops of the dakinis, a supreme legacy

Delightful to all buddhas and bodhisattvas.
For this reason the great gurus of the past
Abandoned all thoughts of danger to body and life
In order to acquire and master them.
Even a speck of this precious doctrine
That matures and frees the mind is rare;
The chariots of the past, with great personal sacrifice,
Gathered the strands of all the instructions
And brought them together as one,
So that now we, without hardship,
Can receive them in accord with our needs;
All from the unfolding of the pure aspirations
And efforts of the great gurus of the past,
Which we should remember until the end of time,
Recollecting them with devotion, rapture and awe.

[As said here, the kindness of the great masters of India and Tibet in preserving and transmitting the Buddhadharma over the centuries is wondrous beyond expression. It is because of the kindness of one's own lama that one receives whatever teachings are necessary for one's spiritual growth and liberation; and it is because of the kindness of the lineage gurus of the past that the precious Dharma has come down to us today without loss of power. One should meditate on this great kindness, and offer supplications with a mind of strong devotion.]

[Thirdly, acknowledging one's personal faults: —]

O Guru Vajradhara and all buddhas, bodhisattvas and arya sangha residing in any of the ten directions, grant me your attention. I, called "Such-and-Such" (state name), in this life and in countless other previous lives since beginningless time, have fallen under the spell of the three kleshas — attachment, anger and confusion — and as a result by means of the doors of body, speech and mind have engaged in the ten negative and unwholesome ways.

I have committed the five most severe negative karmas, and the five almost-as-severe negative karmas.

I have transgressed the guidelines of the way of individual liberation; I have transgressed the trainings of the bodhisattva way; and I have transgressed the precepts of the secret mantra path.

I have shown disrespect to father and mother; I have shown disrespect to spiritual masters and teachers; and I have shown disrespect to friends engaged in pure spiritual ways.

I have engaged in negative deeds that have brought harm to the Three Jewels, have abandoned the spiritual way, have mocked the arya sangha, and have engaged in ways that have harmed other living beings.

By these and other such actions I have created a great mass of negative and unwholesome karma, have encouraged others to do the same, and have rejoiced in seeing others do.

In brief, through these activities I have only created hindrances to my own happiness and freedom, and planted in my path the seeds of my own downfall and pain.

Whatever mass of negative karma and failings exists within me, I face up to it in the presence of the great Guru Vajradhara, as well as all buddhas, bodhisattvas and arya sangha that exist in any of the ten directions. I acknowledge it; I expose it; I do not avoid it; I do not hide from it; and I resolve to transcend it in future. Through acknowledging and exposing it, the process of moving toward inner peace and growth is begun; without acknowledging and exposing it, this simply does not occur.

[*Recite this liturgy three times.*]

[Fourthly, the remaining four limbs of the seven-limbed devotion: —]

I, from time without beginning,
Overpowered by karmic forces and delusion,
Through the doors of body, speech and mind
Have performed many deeds in conflict with goodness
And again and again lost the three spiritual ways.

Contemplating these many failings,
My mind is filled with regret.
In the presence of the holy beings
I acknowledge and resolve to transcend them.

In the marvelous deeds of the gurus, and
The meritorious presence of the buddhas,
Bodhisattvas, pratyekabuddhas, and shravaka arhats,
As well as the goodness in every living being,
I lift up my heart and rejoice.

O all-kind gurus and accomplished buddhas,
In order to mature and liberate the living beings,
I request you to turn the wheel of Dharma
Of the vast and profound instructions.

For as long as a living being remains in samsara,
Do not enter into parinirvana, but remain in this world
And fulfill the needs of living beings;
With the palms of my hands touching at my heart
I send this request to you.

Until the state of enlightenment is achieved,
I turn constantly for inspiration and refuge
To the all-kind gurus, the buddhas,
The Dharma and the community of the arya sangha.

To achieve the state of perfect enlightenment
As a means of becoming most useful in this world,
I give rise to bodhichitta, the mind of universal love,
And resolve to accomplish the bodhisattva trainings.

Through the meritorious energy of this practice
Combined with all other merits that exist,
May I quickly achieve the state of perfect buddhahood
In order best to benefit all that exists.

I myself will follow in the footsteps
Of the great buddhas and bodhisattvas of the past;
The meritorious energy of my doing this, combined
With all other good energies that exist,
I take and dedicate now to the benefit of the world.

[Read these verses while pursuing the according contemplations.]

[If as a peripheral practice you want to renew any precepts that have been
weakened, do so here with the standard liturgies, such as "Om! The lord of
yogis...," which is used for the twenty-eight precepts; or "Just as the masters
in all three times...," which is used to renew the precepts of the five buddha
families. Either liturgy is equally appropriate. However, if instead you wish
to use an abbreviated liturgy, the following will serve the purpose: —]

Just as the buddhas and bodhisattvas of the past
As well as the knowledge holders, dakas and dakinis,
Cultivated an ocean of precepts and trainings
On outer, inner and secret levels,
From now on I will take up that great path,
And for the benefit of all living beings
Resolve to maintain the precepts and trainings.

[*Repeat three times.*]

[Thirdly, offering spiritual aspirations. This begins with a general prayer to
the gurus: —]

The buddhas and their progeny of the ten directions,
To benefit the unprotected beings in this dark age,
Emanate as living beings to work for the good of the world.
Such is the nature of the guru.
I call out to them, the masters carrying out
The works of the buddhas.

I call to the lamas of the three transmissions:
Samantabhadra, Vajrasattva, Garab Dorje, Shri Singha,
Padmakara and his twenty-five great disciples,
So, Zur, Nub and Nyang,
And the hundred treasure revealors.

I call to Buddha Shakyamuni, supreme guide
To the beings of this fortunate age;
To Maitreya and Manjushri; to Nagarjuna, Asanga and his brother
    Vasubandhu;
To the crown ornaments of the Indian masters,
Together with their wondrous disciples,
And to Shantarakshita and Serlingpa.

I call to Buddha Vajradhara, Vajrapani and Lokeshvara,
To the primordial eight mahasiddhas,
And to the eighty-four mahasiddha yogis,
Especially Luhipa, Krishnacharya, Ghantapada and Virupa,
Who attained mastery of the tantric way.

I call to the kings and ministers who were emanations:
Songtsen Gampo, who was Lokeshvara,
Tumi Sambhota, who was Manjushri, the Wheel of Doctrine,
And the Vajrapani emanation [Gar Tongtsen],
Who assisted King Songtsen Gampo (in establishing Dharma in Tibet).

I call to the three whose kindness was immeasurable:
Shantarakshita, an emanation of Vajrapani;
Acharya Padma Sambhava, an emanation of Lokeshvara;
And the Dharma King Trisong Deutsen, emanation of Manjushri.

I call to the ten great pillars of the teaching lineages:
Jamgon Tumi, Bero, Ka, Chok, Zhang, Pelgyi Dorje,
The two great translators Rinchen Zangpo and Ngok Lotsawa,
Sakya Panchen and Buton Rinchen Drup.

I call to the great guru Nyak Lotsawa, who was
Perfected in the four rivers of tantric empowerments;
Nubchen and Ma Lotsawa, great chariots of the sutra and tantra
    doctrines;
The (three great) Zurpa patriarchs — Zur (Shakya Jungney), Mey
(Sherab Drakpa) and Oen (Dropupa), masters of the dakini teachings;
And I call to the chariots of the treasure tradition.

I call to the lineage gurus of the transmissions
In the Old and New Kadampa Schools:
Glorious Atisha, with his disciples Khu, Ngok and Drom;
Drom's spiritual heirs, called "The Three Kadam Brothers"
[Potowa, Chenngawa and Puchungpa] —
And Tsongkhapa, incarnation of Manjushri, with his lineages of
    successors.

I call to the gurus of the Lam Drey transmission:
To the first five generations of Sakya throne-holders;
To Ngorchen, Zongpa and Tsarchen, fathers and sons;
And to the learned and accomplished masters who upheld
Their lineages over the generations to follow.

I call to the gurus of the Dvakpo Kargyu transmission:
To the great Buddha Vajradhara, Tilopa and Naropa;
To Marpa Lotsawa, Milarepa and the venerable Gampopa;
And to the countless mahasiddhas who were to follow
In the four older and eight younger Kargyu schools.

I call to the gurus of the Shangpa school:
To Jnanadakini, Khyungpo Naljor, and the masters
In the lineage of seven jewels* and two rosaries,
That was transmitted through the gurus
In the Close Lineage, such as Tangtong Gyalpo.

[*Vajradhara, Niguma, Khyungpo Naljor, Morchokpa, Kyerkhangpa,
Sanggyey Nyenton, and Sanggyey Tonpa.]

I call to the gurus of the Zhijey and Chod lineages:
Padampa Sangyey and the yogini Machik Labdron;
The three masters Ma, So and Kam;
The four yogis who were gateways; and
All the masters of the early, middle and later
Periods of the Tsar Chod Zhichey transmissions.

I call to the gurus of the Six Kalachakra Yogas:
To the Shambhala kings, and the two Kalachakrapadas;
To Rva, Dro, Tsami Lotsawa, Rangjung, and Dolpopa;
And to the supreme sage Buton Rinchen Drup and his successors.

I call to the gurus of the Nyendrup tradition:
To the supreme adepts of the Six Yogas,
Such as Dorje Tsunmo, Khedrup Orgyenpa,
Rangjung Dorje, Kharchu Putrapa and Nairingpa.

I call to the gurus of the pratimoksha transmissions:
To Buddha Shakyamuni, Shariputra and Rahula;
To the brahmin monk [Saraha], Nagarjuna and his disciples;
And to Shantarakshita and Shakya Shri, transmitters
Of the earlier and later pratimoksha lines.

I call to the gurus of the bodhichitta transmission:
To the bodhisattvas Manjushri and Maitreya;
To Nagarjuna, Shantideva, Asanga and Vasubandhu;
And to Atisha Dipamkara and Kunkhyen Chojey.

I call to those who hold the tantra and practice lineages:
Samantabhadra, Vajradhara, the five tathagatas and three bodhisattvas;
To Gyalpo Dza, Lilavajra and Buddhaguhya;
And to Padmasambhava, the eight knowledge-holders, and Vimala.

I call to the chariots of the tantric lineages:
To Indrabhuti, Virupa and Saraha;
To Luhipa, Krishnacharya and Ghantapada;
And to the eight mahasiddhas and eighty-four yogis.

I call to the all-kind root gurus,
Embodiments of all the traditions:
The Great Treasure Revealer (Terdak Lingpa),
And his brother (Lochen Dharmashri),
Khyentse Wangpo, chariot of Buddha's Rimey legacy,
And Guna (Jamgon Kongtrul the Great), lord of all doctrines.

Send forth your empowering blessings,
That I and all others from now until buddhahood
May be guided by qualified spiritual masters;
That we may maintain the pratimoksha,
Bodhisattva and secret mantra trainings with purity;
And that we may without mistake or error
Enter into the gateways of knowledge.

Send forth your empowering blessings,
That wisdom in the ten arts and sciences may increase;
That the ideas and meditations of the
Sutra and tantra teachings may take effect;
That we may rest in awareness of utter simplicity,
A path that most delights the buddhas;
And that we may learn to understand
How all various ways are without contradiction.

Send forth your empowering blessings,
That I may progress through all the levels of practice:
From that of the basic foundations of three lam rim trainings,
To receiving the four ripening tantric empowerments,
Maintaining pure tantric samaya, cultivating
The generation and completion stage yogas,
And entering the stage of great union itself.

Especially, may the bodhichitta spirit,
The aspiration to be of universal good,
Grow deep from within the depth of my heart;
May I use body, speech and mind only to benefit
Enlightenment and living beings;
May I contribute to the spirit
Of unbiased study and thought; and may
The two goals naturally be achieved.

[That, and also: —]

Eh-ma! I call to incomparable Buddha Shakyamuni,
Who is praised as being a white lotus;
To the successive masters in his precious sutra and tantra lineages;
And to all the masters through whom the lineages descended
In India, Tibet, China, Shambhala and elsewhere.

I call to the Nyingmapa mantrika gurus:
To the holders of the lineages of the general teachings
On the sutras and tantras, and on the three inner tantras,
That were well-translated by supreme lotsawas and pandits
Who had achieved excellence in both learning and practice;
And especially I call to the holders
Of the *dzogchen* "great perfection" tradition.

I call to the Kargyu gurus, protectors of living beings:
To the mahasiddhas Naropa and Maitripa,
From whom descend the profound instruction cycle
And especially the mahamudra lineages;
And to the masters of the successive generations
In this lineage blessed with great practice.

I call to the glorious Sakyapa gurus:
To the masters who illuminated the teaching
That were the heart-essence of mahasiddha Virupa,
The general doctrines and especially that of Lam Drey.

I call to the gurus of Tsongkhapa's tradition,
To the Riwo Gandenpa masters, who hold the lineages
Of the Lam Rim legacy from glorious Atisha,
That makes actual practice its principal focus,
And incorporates all the key trainings
Of both the sutra and tantra paths.

I call to the great guru Jetsun Jonangpa
And to the yogis who followed in his lineage,
Who fused the teachings of the sutras
From Buddha's third turning of the Wheel
With the quintessential teachings of Kalachakra
And found certainty in the meaning of buddhanature.

I call to the masters of all other Tibetan traditions
Holding profound lineages of instruction,
Such as those of the glorious Shangpa, as well as those
Of the Tsarchod Zhijey and the Nyendrup legacies.

O all-kind gurus, heed my call;
Send forth your empowering blessings,
That all disharmony may fade from this world
And the flame of harmony blaze with joy.
May all spiritual leaders be of one mind,
May happiness everywhere pervade the land,
And may the enlightenment teachings thrive and spread.

[The above is in accordance with the Rimey tradition. If you want to add
a small liturgy exclusive to the Nyingma School, which is of the earlier
dissemination, the following can be used: —]

Eh ma hoh!
I call to the teachers of the three kayas:
Buddha Samantabhadra, endowed with six special characteristics;
Vajrasattva, great bliss with seven branches of union;
And Vajrapani, who abides under their mysterious command.

I call to the five types of knowledge holders
Who elucidated the quintessential path of the eighteen tantras,
Such as that sun amongst orators Licchavi Vimalakirti,
And to the devas, nagas, yakshas and rakshas.

I call to all the accomplished adepts:
To Gyalpo Dza, a chariot carrying an ocean of tantric teachings,
The eight knowledge holders who revealed profound treasures,
And Garab Dorje, lord of the supreme Dzogchen vehicle.

I call to all the mighty yogis and yoginis,
To Padma Sambhava, embodiment of the buddhas of the three times,
His nine heart-disciples, with whom he had strong karmic links, and to
The twenty-one appointed ones and twenty-five subjects.

I call to the lineage masters and their disciples:
To Ma, Nyak and Nub, on whom fell the three yogas;
To the three Zurpa patriarchs,
Who were like incarnations of Vajrapani himself;
And to the three suns amongst teachers,
Rongzom Mahapandita, Longchenpa and Nyo Tonpa.

Hear my call and bestow blessings of the three kayas.
O knowledge holders, empower myself and all others
With the empowerments that mature and liberate;
Bestow the siddhis of the four types of vidyadharas.
Bestow your blessings for quick progress in practice,
That I may succeed in seeing my skandhas and ayadanas as mandala
    deities;
That I may succeed in the yoga of channels, subtle energies and drops;
That I may experience the great melting in the central channel;
And that I may take the four visions to the end
And achieve the fulfillment of the two goals.

[The above is an example of a prayer to the lineage gurus of a particular
school, in this case the Nyingma. It can be replaced with a liturgy for the
lineage of gurus of the school with which you have the closest affiliation.]

[Secondly, invoking the guru's attention by means of recitation of his mantra: —]

At the heart of Jamgon Lama Khyentse Wangpo is the Wisdom Being, in nature all buddhas, the glorious Vajradharma, his guise that of glorious Heruka, holding a damaru drum and skull cup filled with wine, a katvanga staff resting over his shoulder, on a lotus and sun, his feet in the posture of vajra play.

At his heart is a lotus and moon seat, and on it the syllable HUM, surrounded by knowledge-holding gurus.

Lights emanate from HUM, attracting the attention of the surrounding gurus. The radiance of the great vajra wisdom of their body, speech and mind fills the world of universe and living beings, arousing the great purity of their mandalas of body, speech and mind.

As a response to my strong request to the gurus, a great rain of blessings pours down onto myself, others, and all living beings.

Om ah guru Manjugosha sarva siddhi hum.

[Recite this, the name mantra of the guru, many times in order to invoke his blessings.]

[Then recite the general name mantra, which is dedicated to all the other masters in the field of visualization: —]

Om ah hum maha guru sarva siddhih hum.

[Thirdly, making requests to fulfill aspirations and needs: —]

Precious guru, embodiment of all objects of refuge,
Your form a reflection of the wisdom of all buddhas,
An all-embracing lord of all profound mysteries
Manifested as an ordinary human teacher for those like me,
Master who opens our eyes to the door of freedom
By showing what needs transcending and what (needs) cultivation,
Thus revealing the unmistaken path that leads
To the jewel land of enlightenment itself,
Indeed your kindness to me is more wondrous
Than that of all buddhas and bodhisattvas.

I send this request to you:
Establish my mind in the ways of the sages;
Correct any errors in practice that I make;
Remove obstacles and hindrances from my path;
Direct me to the city of the four buddha kayas.

O gurus, when the good boat of universal love
That flies the flag of sublime detachment
Is moved by the wind of spiritual concern,
Arise in the form of the two bodhichittas
And pass on the power of inner liberation.

O gurus, when the mind has been ripened with the four
    empowerments,
The instructions on the sutra and tantra paths been received,
And meditation on the outer and inner generation stage
As well as on the three paths has met with success,
O great gurus, at that time
Arise in the form of the four buddha kayas and
Be a bridge to the ground of the stage beyond training.

When efforts to reverse worldly fixations
Become insight that perceives the real nature of being,
And both energy and mind by interdependent arisings
Flow into *avadhuti*, the central channel,
O gurus, arise in the form of innate primordial awareness
And push my practice of the four yogas to the end.

When the quick path of method and liberation is established
And the clear light level of mind spontaneously appears,
O gurus, arise in the form of dharmakaya's simplicity
And bestow the blessing of liberation in one lifetime.

When the mindstream has been ripened by the practices
Of the interdependent paths of sutra and tantra,
And outer and inner obstacles seen as dharmakaya,
O gurus, arise in the form of a great pacifier
And take my realization of higher wisdom to the end.

When meditation on the method of resting the mind
And energies in the central channel dhuti
Is applied with the six vajra yoga applications,
O gurus, arise in pure outer, inner and other forms,
And reveal the wonders of the ten yogic signs.

When the three doors, energies, drops and mind
Have been brought to rest in the three eternal vajras,
O gurus, arise in the form of three vajras
And push me to the end of the nyendrup yogas.

When within the sphere of primordially pure dharmakaya,
The timeless wisdom present even in confusion,
Clear light and the four glorious visions are known,
O gurus, arise in the form of a great wisdom master
And dissolve my mind into the space of the void.

From now until the essence of enlightenment has been gained,
When high and when low, when happy and when sad,
May I never be parted from awareness of the gurus
And always be cared for by them;
And may I receive the blessings that lead to siddhi.

First one meets with the guru in conventional external aspect
And is placed in the door of the unmistaken Dharma path;
In the middle one meets with a truly learned and accomplished guru
In rimey aspect, and through study and contemplation discovers
The meaning of the liberation of the mind;
And in the end one meets with the Lord of the World Guru,
And experiences an unbroken stream of great purity wisdom.
May I be always cared for by that dharmakaya guru of final essence
      awareness,
And be led to the city of the non-dual four kayas.

May the gurus who give the four tantric initiations
Heal essence, elements and powers;
May the gurus who give the oral instructions
Reveal the path of method and liberation;
May the resultant guru bestow the royal method
Of the four perfect buddha kayas;
And may living beings experience the glory
Of the two goals being spontaneously fulfilled.

May the rebirth/nirmanakaya guru induce experience of the path
And awaken perception of all appearing phenomena
As deities, all sounds as mantra, and all thoughts as dharmakaya;
May the death/dharmakaya guru point out suchness itself
And blend mother and child clear lights into one;
And may the bardo/samboghakaya guru turn the world into a buddhafield
That merely seeing, hearing of or thinking about
Places one on the primordial ground itself.

The Concluding Activities

[If you want to perform a torma offering to the Dharma Protectors, you can do so in either an elaborate or a brief form, inserting the practice here. Use whatever liturgy is appropriate to the specific practice.]

[The first of the concluding activities is that of the tantric feast. Take whatever foods and drinks are to be used and arrange them on the table. Sprinkle a few drops of vase water and inner offering nectar (from the skull cup) in the direction of the feast substances to consecrate them, and chant as follows]

RAM. YAM. KHAM. From the sphere of emptiness appear air and fire mandalas, with a tripod of three human skulls above them, and above that an enormous skull cup, inside of which are the feast substances in the form of the five meats and five nectars. Air moves; fire rises; all the substances in the skull cup melt and boil. They are completely purified; their color, fragrance, taste, power and nutrient become fabulous, and they transform into a vast ocean of the nectar of non-samsaric wisdom. Om ah hum!

[The invocation of the field of merit: —]

> The nature of the guru pervades everything in samsara and nirvana
> And manifests in accordance with the needs of trainees;
> O gurus, yidams, buddhas, bodhisattvas,
> Dakas, dakinis, Dharma protectors and others,
> Come to this place to facilitate our merit and wisdom.
>
> Come in joyous bodies performing vajra dance,
> With speech speaking Dharma, reciting verse, and singing vajra songs,
> With mind beyond conceptuality in bliss and radiance,
> And with wisdom performing inconceivable magic deeds.
> Release a great rain of empowerments and siddhis.
> Sarve samaya jah jah.

[Now take the first portion of the feast substances and offer it in honor of the guru and Three Roots: —]

> Om ah hum hoh.
> This non-samsaric feast, a cloud of wisdom nectar,
> Supreme substances as divinely sensual ambrosia,
> I offer to the spiritual masters of the Kadam tradition.
> Inspire me to arouse the supreme mind of bodhichitta.
>
> Om ah hum hoh.
> This non-samsaric offering, a cloud of wisdom nectar,
> Supreme samaya substances that are the five buddha families and five
> wisdoms,
> I offer to the assembly of (Sakya) yogis,
> Who uphold the lineage of the secret Lam Drey teaching.
> Inspire me to take the practice
> Of the four empowerments to the end.
>
> Om ah hum hoh.
> This non-samsaric offering, a cloud of wisdom nectar,
> Supreme substances that are the method and wisdom of great vajra bliss,
> I offer to the ocean of (Kargyu and Shangpa) mahasiddhas.
> Inspire me to complete the supreme path
> Of method and liberation combined.
>
> Om ah hum hoh.
> This non-samsaric feast, a cloud of wisdom nectar,
> Supreme substances that are purified vajra skandhas and dhatus,
> I offer to the mahasiddhas of the Kalachakra and Nyendrup traditions.
> Inspire me to accomplish the six yogic applications
> And the Nyendrup tantric doctrines.

Om ah hum hoh.
This non-samsaric feast, a cloud of wisdom nectar,
Supreme substances that are an offering cloud
Of clear light mind with the six lamps and four visions,
I offer to the (Nyingma) gurus who reveal the supreme tantric path.
Inspire me to accomplish the vajra siddhi
Of the rainbow body in which all stains are exhausted.

[Partake of the feast. Afterwards, make an offering of the extra: —]

Om ah hum ha hoh hrih. [...to consecrate.]

Eh aralli pem [...summons the guests for the extra.]

Om ah hum hoh.
This non-samsaric feast, a cloud of wisdom nectar,
I offer to the external Dharma protectors, such as
The Dorje Ginlang Protectors and Wangchukma Guardians,*
To the inner protectors, such as the dakas and dakinis of the sacred
    places,
And to the secret protectors, the Wisdom Lords.
Perform the enlightenment activity of fulfilling my wishes.
Om uchhi shada balimta kha hi.

[*The sixteen Dorje Ginlang Protectors and twenty-eight Wangchukma
Guardians."]

Knowledge holder, guru who is like the Three Roots,
I make you an offering of this tantric feast.
May it cause me and all other living beings
To accomplish the sacred mandala as one.

[If in order to strengthen merit and purify negative karma you want to do a counted number of recitations of the above, then begin from the passage, "With my palms pressed together above the crown of my head, / My fingers together like the petals of a flower bud, / Like upstretched petals of a young lotus in a beautiful pool, / I give melodious voice...." One repeats the section beginning from there until the verse ending above.

Alternatively, one can do a set number of recitations of any other prayer, such as "The Prayer to the Twenty-five Great Tibetan Masters," that begins with the words, "Acharya Padma Sambhava, embodiment of the Three Roots...." One can also recite "The Prayer of Individual Purification and Three Mantras"; or any of the prayers to the individual great masters. These can be inserted here.

Perhaps conclude with omniscient [Jamgon Kongtrul] Lodro Tayey's "Prayer for the Spread of the Rimey Tradition," which begins with the words, "More than the thousand buddhas of the auspicious age...."]

[Secondly, the thanksgiving offering. Freshen the offering bowls on the altar by adding a small extra portion to each, sprinkle water from the vase, do the "offering cloud" mantra, and then chant as follows: —]

I pay homage to the myriad gurus
Who deliver the gift of benefit and joy;
Merely thinking of you or remembering your names
Cuts the flow of worldly and spiritual apathy.

All things that delight gods, nagas, rakshas and humans,
And even those that delight all bodhisattvas in the ten directions,
I offer to the guru, embodiment of the refuge objects,
Lord in the world when it comes to spiritual knowledge.
I request you to accept this offering.

To all spiritual forces in all directions
Who bring goodness in all four times,*
I bow in homage and offer devotion;
In their presence I freely face all failings,
Rejoice in all goodness, request the turning of the Dharma Wheel,
Request the gurus to remain for a hundred aeons,
And dedicate all merit to other living beings.

[*Past, present and future, with the fourth being all three
    simultaneously experienced as one flow.]

[The above verse contains all seven limbs of the seven-limbed devotion.]

[Thirdly, taking the four tantric empowerments. A somewhat expanded
liturgy for the process of this meditation is as follows. First offer the mandala,
and then place the palms of your hands together and chant as follows: —]

> Homage to all-encompassing lord of all buddha families.
> My quest is the great path of liberation,
> And I ask for empowerment and sacred samaya.
> I turn to you for inspiration and guidance.
> Place me in the house of the Supreme Way;
> Bestow knowledge and primordial wisdom upon me.

[One recites this verse three times. Then: —]

Requested in this way, the entourage gurus all radiate with joy and dissolve
into light, which then melts into Jamgon Lama Khyentse Wangpo, the lord
of all buddha families.

From the heart of the guru, embodiment of all spiritual forces and
lord of the four buddha kayas, the empowerment deities of the complete
three seats emanate forth, until all the skies are filled. The knowledge
goddesses come forth in auspicious style; and then, holding up vases filled
with wisdom essence, they sing the following lines as they pour forth their
nectars of empowerment: —

> Hum! This great and auspicious vase
> Is the mansion of those gone to bliss.
> With it you are given supreme empowerment
> Into a most wondrous and complete mandala.
> Om vajra kalasha abhishicha hum.

Singing this verse, a river of empowerment nectar flows forth, completely
filling my body. The stains of the five kleshas are purified, I am authorized
to meditate on the generation stage yogas, and the destiny to attain the
resultant nirmanakaya is established.

With a pressing tone I again request empowerment. In response, syllables emanate from the scripture containing vast doors of Dharma, which is in the lotus beside Jamgon Lama Khyentse Wangpo's left shoulder, the stem of which he holds in the fingers of his left hand. Each of these tiny syllables of the Sanskrit alphabet emits its own sound. This stream of tiny syllables comes to the crown of my head and descends to the center of my heart, where it is absorbed. I receive the empowering blessing of the ability to discuss, debate and write about anything in the vast ocean of tantric scriptures, just as did the two supreme masters and the six ornament pandits of ancient India, and the masters of the ten great teaching lineages in Tibet.

A great treasure of unfading wisdom and confidence in Dharma is aroused within me, and I become Dorje Nonpo, the bodhisattva who is a lion's roar among Dharma teachers for those ready to be trained.

> May I receive the empowerment of the sutra and tantra scriptures,
> An oceanic field of profound significance,
> A sublime peace of incomparable character,
> Good in the beginning, middle and end.
> Om dharma sara abhishicha hum.

[Recite the syllables and the mantra of dependent origination.]

Manjushri Lama Jamgon Khyentse Wangpo hears my supplication, and from his right hand a river of empowering wisdom nectars flow forth, entering my body via my crown aperture. My body becomes filled by the flow of nectar. I receive the blessings of the four empowerments and three vajras, and of the eighty-four mahasiddhas of ancient India and the masters of the eight great practice lineages in Tibet. The qualities of the four paths are made manifest just as they are. I am empowered to study, meditate upon and practice the way of profound mysteries. I receive the complete empowerment and blessing with the capacity to accomplish all stages of the path that fulfills the two purposes, and become of one nature with Buddha Vajrapani, the Lord of Secret Ways.

May I receive profoundly mysterious empowerment,
That manifests a net of magical activities,
Deep and vast in its oceanic nature,
Great in its power to benefit living beings.
Om mantra guhya abhishicha hum.

[Again recite the syllables and the mantra of dependent origination.]

The guru arises in the sambhogakaya form of Buddha Vajradhara in union
with his consort. The two enter into sexual union. A drop of the bodhichitta
substances that flow, in nature an embodiment of all the buddhas, is placed
on the tip of my tongue.

Hum. To bestow the empowerment a drop is placed on your tongue,
A drop of white (male) and red (female) supreme bodhichitta
That is able to satiate in every way,
The great bodhichitta of pleasure and joy,
Om vajra guhya abhishicha hum.

The nectar is offered in this way. I recite *om ah hum*, and ingest it. The
samadhi of the non-conceptual wisdom of radiance and emptiness arises,
and bestows the secret empowerment. All negative karmic instincts caused
by acts of speech are purified, I am authorized to meditate on the path of
subtle energies, chakras and channels, and the destiny to accomplish the
resultant samboghakaya is established.

A knowledge maiden emanates forth from the guru's heart, perfect
in form and age, in essence Vajra Dakini. The urge to rely upon liberation
becomes strong.

This maiden, this wondrous mudra,
Is the bestower of limitless bliss
And has all the skills of a consort.
O son, make the peerless offering.
Om vajra prajna jnana abhishicha hum.

Maintaining the three awarenesses, I enter into union with the mudra. The four joys arise, and induce experience of semblent clear light wisdom. Om sarva tathagata anuragana vajra svabhava atma ko ham.

The wisdom awareness empowerment is received, stains of the mind are purified, and I am authorized to meditate on the path of the drops. The destiny to accomplish the resultant dharmakaya is established.

From the vajra and bell of the Jamgon Lama Khyentse Wangpo, and from the heart of the mandala deity, who is inseparably one with the mass of male and female accomplished vidyadharas, there emanate forth the peaceful and wrathful mandala deities, who are blessed with the seal of the wisdom of bliss and void. All take the form of glorious Vajrasattva, the solitary lord of all buddha families, who then melts into my heart. My body becomes that of the deity, speech becomes mantra, and mind becomes wisdom; in this way my body, speech and mind become inseparably one with the ornamental wheel of the eternal three mysteries of the myriad mandala deities. I achieve the empowerment, together with all blessings and siddhis.

> Om ah hum.
> Holding the form of a glorious buddha,
> Lord of the three inseparable vajras,
> Right now receive the empowerment
> Of the body, speech and mind of all buddhas.
> Om vajra prajna kaya vaga chitta abhishicha om ah hum.

To fulfill the fourth empowerment, the great Guru Vajradhara bestows it simply by means of words.

> This extremely subtle primordial awareness,
> Like the space of vajra essence,
> Is beyond matter, a thing of peace,
> The quintessential nature of being itself.
> Om vajra dharma dhatu abhishicha ah.

Empowering blessings flow forth, arousing the direct experience of the inconceivable ultimate nature of being, the wisdom of dharmata itself, which spontaneously understands all realities. This bestows the fourth empowerment. All stains on the wisdom mind are purified, and one is authorized to meditate on *dzogpa chenpo*, the great perfection. The destiny to attain the resultant svabhavakaya is established.

[Again make a mandala offering.]

[If you want to abbreviate the above liturgy, it is acceptable just to chant the passages on the emanating and workings of the light rays and nectar, and to omit the rest of the text.]

[Fourthly, the yoga of the absorption: —]

"Guru Vajradhara, embodiment of all spiritual forces,
Be inseparably with me until my enlightenment is won;
Be with me in my physical actions, words and thoughts,
And arouse the primordial wisdom in my spirit.
Bestow empowerment, blessings and siddhi on me."

This said, the guru dissolves into light, which melts into me.
His mind and mine become as one, complete with his vast and playful
    vision.
Within this sphere of primordial awareness of all in the three times,
I directly see the face of the dharmakaya,
The clear light state that is beyond the conceptual mind.

[Having recited these words, rest in the sphere of silence for awhile.]

[When the time comes to conclude the session, do so by chanting the
following prayer: —]

Through any meritorious energy created by this practice,
May I and all other living beings
Be cared for continually by a master of the sacred wheel.
By following pure samaya with certainty and a joyous heart,
May we quickly gain the stage of the supreme masters.

I call to the incomparable Jetsun Jamgon Lama Khyentse Wangpo,
Embodiment of Buddha Shakyamuni and his disciples,
And of Samantabhadra, Vajradhara, and
The Three Jewels and Three Roots, as well as of the
Myriad of dakas, dakinis and Dharma protectors:
Look on me from the primordial perfection of your three mysteries.

Cultivating clarity, sublime detachment, compassion and wisdom,
And dwelling in spiritual awareness of the Three Jewels
Together with the perspective of universal concern,
May I cultivate the path pleasing to the buddhas,
Beginning with the common, uncommon and special preliminaries.

Ultimately all things have emptiness as their final nature, yet
Conventionally they function as dependent arisings,
And always arise from within the sphere
That is motionless and beyond aspirations:
May I realize this middle view of the supreme way
That is free from all extremes.

May I dwell in awareness of the three ways
Of resting the mind in its natural state,
And gain the samadhi of the four buddha kayas
Through the four yogas that experience the four faults as self-liberated.
Thus may I fulfill mahamudra meditation.

Striking to the very core the magical display
Of projections, basic awareness and emptiness
With visualization, mantra and the quick path of methodology and
    freedom,
May all experiences, both happy and sad, be drawn into the path,
And everything in samsara and nirvana made to arise as dharmakaya.
Through constantly living in the one-tasteness of being,
May all hindrances and negative energies instantly be dispelled.

May the mind's habit of distortion and holding things as real
Be liberated in the sphere of primordial purity;
May awareness of the natural processes of things
Cause all imperfections to fade on their own ground;
May I assume a youthful vase-like dharmadhatu form,
And may I realize the four visions of the resultant Great Perfection.

May I myself come to equal the guru, who with
Quick compassion looks on the beings filling space,
Master rich in skillful power for training the beings to be trained,
Great guru who spontaneously fulfills the two goals.

[The concluding "Song of Auspiciousness": —]

May there be auspicious signs of the incomparable guru,
Who leads spiritual practitioners to supreme siddhi,
A precious jewel at the top of the victory banner,
A supreme crown ornament for those beyond the world.

May there be auspicious signs of the blossoming
Of the beautiful garden of the sublime Buddhadharma,
With wisdom as the root, sublime detachment the sap,
And the mind of universal love the nectar spreading out,
With thousands of flower petals opening everywhere
Bearing seekers involved in the three activities
Of study, contemplation and meditation.

May there be the auspicious signs
Of a rainfall of flowers of tantric empowerment,
The summer thunder of teachings on the generation and completion
    stage yogas,
The summer blossoming of the flowers of pure samaya,
And the ripening of the fruit of the three disciplines.

May there be auspicious signs of the certainty of
The pure view of emptiness vast as the sky
Adorned with the sun, moon and stars of clear light meditation;
And of the perfection of the excellences of the path beyond training,
That is attained in this lifetime by means of self-liberated application.

[Thus the practice is concluded.]

Instructions on Adapting the Text for Personal Practice

[The above text contains all the key points for both the guruyoga and guru-puja practices. In general, to use it in accordance with how it is structured here is best.

However, it can also be adapted in various ways. For example, if you want to practice it mainly as a guruyoga method, then have the session mainly be dedicated to a count of recitations of the prayer and also of the name mantra. The rest of the liturgy, especially the seven-limbed devotion and the various types of offerings, can be abbreviated in accordance with circumstance. The various notes in the text should make clear how this is to be done. The important thing in abbreviating the liturgy is to remain clear on the six mindfulnesses.

As for doing a counted number of recitations of a particular prayer, here there are a wide variety of liturgies to draw from, such as the various general prayers extracted from the Indian classics; the specific prayers such as "The Three Vows," "The Eight Masters"; and so forth. Use whatever is your favorite, and chant it the decided number of times.

If you do a large number of recitations of the name mantra, then combine this with frequently repeating the process of taking the empowerments, expanding or abbreviating the liturgy as required for the practice format.

When the practice is mainly being done as a gurupuja (as opposed to a guruyoga), arrange hundreds or even thousands of offerings on the altar, such as flowers, butter lamps, foods, and so forth. Make actual physical prostrations during the appropriate part of the liturgy, and do the offering sections in the elaborate forms (as marked in the text). Also, repeat the mandala offerings many times.]

[Here the main figure in the visualized merit field is Jamyang Khyentse Wangpo, because the very fact that the Rimey Dharma Tradition comes down to us today is due to his kindness.

Jamyang Khyentse Rinpoche himself wrote,

> In brief, I gathered together nearly all transmissions
> Found in any of the ten great teaching lineages,
> Trained in them, and gained some small experience.
> This gave me positive appreciation of their techniques. And also,
> The Early Transmissions, the Old and New Kadampa,
> The Sakyapa Order, the Marpa and Shangpa Kargyupa,
> And the (Kalachakra) transmission of the six yogas, together with
> The Tsarchod Zhijey and Nyendrup traditions.
> These are the eight great practice lineages;
> Honoring all eight, and with the mind of devotion,
> I sought out and acquired their various teachings
> With great personal effort and hardship,
> So that none of them would be lost.

All the great masters of Tibet unanimously describe Khyentse Wangpo as a lama who, by the strength of his knowledge, compassion and power, became a lord of the complete Buddhadharma.

However, if you want to replace him as the central figure in the visualization with a different lama, this can be done. The section of the text with the description of the merit field just has to be adjusted accordingly.

For example, if you would prefer to use the Fifth Dalai Lama as the main figure in the assembly of gurus, the following liturgy can be used: —]

> In the space in front of me there instantly appears
> The lord of all buddha families, holder of the three vajras,
> Gyalwa Lobzang Gyatso, Victorious Ocean of Sublime Thoughts,
> Holder of the White Lotus, seated in a ball of light,
> His face white tinged with red,
> His gaze strong and his eyes wide with compassion,
> His right hand in the mudra of giving refuge,
> The fingers holding the stem of a white lotus
> That unfolds in bloom by his shoulder,

Symbolizing his knowledge, compassion and wisdom;
And his left in the mudra of meditation,
The golden wheel that rests above it
Magically manifesting amazing enlightenment deeds.
His body is clothed in the three robes of a monk, and
He is wearing the golden hat of a Tripitaka holder.

[Taking this as an example, it is easy to see how the liturgy can be edited
to incorporate any alternative Rimey lama as the image at the center of the
visualized assembly.]

[A third alternative is to use one's own root guru, rather than one of the
main lineage masters. A liturgy for this could be as follows: —]

In the space in front of me, on a jewelled throne upheld by lions,
Is my own root guru, master of incomparable kindness,
His form is that of all-encompassing Vajrasattva,
His body white with radiance, like a snow mountain
Struck by the light of a thousand suns.
His face is full with power and with a gentle smile,
And he is adorned with the marks and signs of perfection.
His right hand holds a vajra at his heart,
And his left, which embraces his consort,
Holds a bell at his waist
His two feet crossed in the vajra posture.
His consort, Vajragarvi, is the color of the moon,
She holds a curved knife and a skull cup,
Her arms wrapped around his neck.
They sit in sexual union,
Both of them youthful and clothed in exquisite silks.
There is a blazing and a great blast of light,
And Vajrasattva takes the outer form of the guru,
Displaying nine peaceful modes, he wears an upper robe of white cloth,
His lower robe multicolored like a rainbow,

Crown ribbons, hair ribbons, and scarves for dance,
Thus having all five silken garments.
He is also adorned with the eight jewel ornaments:
The jewel crown, earrings, necklaces, bracelets, anklets,
Belt, crystals and middle and lower necklaces.

Seated amidst a limitless radiance of light,
His nature is that of non-dual bliss and emptiness,
His five skandhas the five buddhas,
His elements the various consorts,
His eight gatherings of consciousness, their organs and objects,
Are the male and female bodhisattvas.
His limbs are the eight annihilating gate keepers in union,
And all the others of the cloud-like display
Of the mandala wheel of peaceful and wrathful deities.

[Then recite the following mantra: —]

Om guru vajrasattva siddhi ah hum.

[This concludes the presentation of the practice.]

Better than devotion to all buddhas and bodhisattvas
Is devotion to a single pore of the guru,
Who gives the priceless jewel of the sutra and tantra instruction;
Inspired by this ancient saying,
I composed this text.

If any meritorious energy comes out of it,
May it be dedicated to the attainment of the state
That is an ornament of the world and beyond,
The stainless jewel of joyous spiritual glory;
And by that force, may I be mindful of the gurus
In all my lives, blending their thoughts with mine,
Working for the good of buddhahood and living beings.

Colophon

When I was fifteen years old there was a gathering of many great masters, including the tantric lord of a hundred lineages, Padma Tenzin Khedrup Gyatso Wangpo Dey (i.e., the Third Sechen Gyaltsap), accompanied by two young Jamgon incarnations (Note: Dzongsar Jamyang Khyentse Chokyi Lodro, 1893-1959, and Shechen Kongtrul Pema Drime, 1901-1960). The lama gave extensive teachings at Zhechen Ritro Demchok Tashi Gepel Monastery on the subject of "The Treasury of Oral Instructions" (an important Rimey compilation). My name, Mangal, appeared on the list of attendees. Because of the kindness of this great master, I developed profound faith in the Buddhist Rimey movement.

Then when I was in my thirty-second year I received signs of a small blessing from (i.e., vision of) the chariots of the eight great practice lineages. I was deeply moved by that experience, and composed a brief guruyoga liturgy focussing on them.

Later Kyabje Zhadeu Trulzhik Choktrul Gyurmey Chokyi Lodro Rinpoche (i.e. Trulshik Tulku), a master who has truly aroused the perfections of the transmission and realization Dharmas within his stream of being, and who is a great upholder of the Rimey tradition, made the request that I compose a lama chopa liturgy for Rimey practitioners.

In response to his entreaty, I took the guruyoga text on the chariots of the eight practice lineages that I had previously composed, and somewhat expanded upon it, basing this on the writings of earlier masters, until it came into its present shape.

The scribe Nying Ngak Gyurmey Kelzang Pelgey assisted me in completing the task. It was composed while I was residing at the Tadul Tsuklakang, Patro Kyerchu, in the Tashi Garkyil meditation hermitage (Bhutan).

May it contribute to enlightenment and happiness, and help bring the blessings of the wisdom of the spiritual masters into the world.

Other books by Glenn H. Mullin

The Tibetan Book of the Dead: An Illustrated Edition, with photos by Thomas Kelly, Roli Books, New Delhi, 2009

Buddha in Paradise: A Celebration in Himalayan Art, Rubin Museum of Art, NY, 2007

The Flying Mystics in Tibetan Buddhist Art, Serindia Publications, Chicago and London, 2006

The Second Dalai Lama: His Life and Teachings, Snow Lion Publications, Ithaca, NY, 2005

Living in the Face of Death, Snow Lion Publications, Ithaca, NY, 2004

The Female Buddhas : Women of Enlightenment in Tibetan Mystical Art, Clear Light Publications, Santa Fe, 2003

The Fourteen Dalai Lamas: A Sacred Legacy of Reincarnation, Clear Light Publications, Santa Fe, 2001

Gems of Wisdom from the Seventh Dalai Lama, Snow Lion Publications, Ithaca, NY, 1999

Readings on the Six Yogas of Naropa, Snow Lion Publications, Ithaca, NY, 1998

Tsongkhapa's Six Yogas of Naropa, Snow Lion Publications, Ithaca, NY, 1997

The Mystical Arts of Tibet, Longstreet Press, Atlanta, 1996

The Dalai Lamas on Tantra, Snow Lion Publications, Ithaca, 1995

Mystical Verses of a Mad Dalai Lama, Quest Books, Chicago, 1994

Training the Mind in the Great Way: A Commentary by the First Dalai Lama, Snow Lion Publications, Ithaca, NY, 1993

The Practice of Kalachakra, Snow Lion Publications, Ithaca, NY, 1991

The Art of Compassion, Tibet House, New Delhi, 1989

Selected Works of the Thirteenth Dalai Lama: Path of the Bodhisattva Warrior, Snow Lion Publications, Ithaca, NY, 1988

Selected Works of the Sixth Dalai Lama: Songs of Love and Laughter, Tushita Books, Dharamsala, India, 1987

Death and Dying : The Tibetan Tradition, Penguin Arcana, London, 1986

Selected Works of the Second Dalai Lama: The Tantric Yogas of Sister Niguma, Snow Lion Publications, Ithaca, NY, 1985

Meditations on the Lower Tantras: Translated Works by the Early Dalai Lamas, Library of Tibetan Works and Archives, Dharamsala, India, 1984

Selected Works of the Third Dalai Lama: Essence of Refined Gold, Snow Lion Publications, Ithaca, NY, 1983
Selected Works of the First Dalai Lama: Bridging the Sutras and Tantras, Snow Lion Publications, Ithaca, NY,, 1982

Selected Works of the Seventh Dalai Lama: Songs of Spiritual Change, Snow Lion Publications, Ithaca, NY, 1981

Six Texts Related to the Tara Tantra, from the Works of the First Dalai Lama, Tibet House, New Delhi, 1980

Atisha and Buddhism in Tibet, Tibet House, New Delhi, 1979

The Practice of Vajrabhairava, Tushita Books, India, 1979

Lama Mipam's Commentary to Nagarjuna's Stanzas for a Novice Monk, Library of Tibetan Works and Archives, Dharamsala, India, 1978

Four Songs to Jey Rinpoche, Library of Tibetan Works and Archives, Dharamsala, India, 1977